This book belongs to:

....

Southern Living

LITTLE JARS, BIG FLAVORS

Small-batch jams, jellies, pickles,
and preserves from the South's
most trusted kitchen

Oxmoor
HOUSE®

ISBN-13: 978-0-8487-3952-2
ISBN-10: 0-8487-3952-3
Library of Congress Control Number: 2013930595

Printed in the United States of America
First Printing 2013

Oxmoor House
Editorial Director: Leah McLaughlin
Creative Director: Felicity Keane
Senior Brand Manager: Daniel Fagan
Senior Editor: Rebecca Brennan
Managing Editor: Rebecca Benton

Southern Living Little Jars, Big Flavors
Editor: Nichole Aksamit
Art Director: Claire Cormany
Project Editor: Emily Chappell
Senior Designer: Melissa Clark
Director, Test Kitchen: Elizabeth Tyler Austin
Assistant Directors, Test Kitchen: Julie Christopher, Julie Gunter
Recipe Developers and Testers: Wendy Ball, R.D.; Victoria E. Cox; Tamara Goldis; Stefanie Maloney; Callie Nash; Karen Rankin; Leah Van Deren
Recipe Editor: Alyson Moreland Haynes
Food Stylists: Margaret Monroe Dickey, Catherine Crowell Steele
Photography Director: Jim Bathie
Senior Photographer: Hélène Dujardin
Senior Photo Stylist: Kay E. Clarke
Photo Stylist: Mindi Shapiro Levine
Assistant Photo Stylist: Mary Louise Menendez
Senior Production Manager: Susan Chodakiewicz
Production Manager: Theresa Beste-Farley

Contributors
Writer: Virginia Willis
Designer: Cathy Robbins
Recipe Developers and Testers: Tonya Johnson, Kyra Moncrief
Copy Editor: Donna Baldone
Proofreaders: Dolores Hydock, Rhonda Lee Lother
Indexer: Mary Ann Laurens
Interns: Morgan Bolling, Susan Kemp, Sara Lyon, Staley McIlwain, Emily Robinson, Maria Sanders, Katie Strasser
Food Stylist: Kathleen Royal Phillips
Photographers: Becky Luigart-Stayner, Ellen Silverman, Daniel Taylor
Photo Stylist: Lydia DeGaris Pursell

Southern Living®
Editor: M. Lindsay Bierman
Creative Director: Robert Perino
Managing Editor: Candace Higginbotham
Art Director: Chris Hoke
Executive Editors: Rachel Hardage Barrett, Hunter Lewis, Jessica S. Thuston
Food Director: Shannon Sliter Satterwhite
Test Kitchen Director: Rebecca Kracke Gordon
Senior Writer: Donna Florio
Senior Food Editor: Mary Allen Perry
Recipe Editor: JoAnn Weatherly
Assistant Recipe Editor: Ashley Arthur
Test Kitchen Specialist/Food Styling: Vanessa McNeil Rocchio
Test Kitchen Professionals: Norman King, Pam Lolley, Angela Sellers
Senior Photographers: Ralph Lee Anderson, Gary Clark, Art Meripol
Photographers: Robbie Caponetto, Laurey W. Glenn
Photo Research Coordinator: Ginny P. Allen
Senior Photo Stylist: Buffy Hargett
Editorial Assistant: Pat York

Time Home Entertainment Inc.
Publisher: Jim Childs
VP, Strategy & Business Development: Steven Sandonato
Executive Director, Marketing Services: Carol Pittard
Executive Director, Retail & Special Sales: Tom Mifsud
Director, Bookazine Development & Marketing: Laura Adam
Executive Publishing Director: Joy Butts
Associate Publishing Director: Megan Pearlman
Finance Director: Glenn Buonocore
Associate General Counsel: Helen Wan

CONTENTS

LIKE MANY SOUTHERNERS,
I GREW UP WITH CANNING AND PRESERVING.

My family always planted a large kitchen garden near the house and often kept another plot for corn in the fertile soil down by the river. We ate food fresh in season and preserved the garden's goodness for later too. My mother and grandmother taught me to freeze black-eyed peas, butterbeans, and creamed corn; to transform peaches, wild blackberries, and Scuppernong grapes into jams and jellies; to can green beans and tomatoes in summer; and to put up peanuts, pears, and spicy chowchow in the fall. They showed me how sliced cucumbers became bread-and-butter pickles and how quartered cucumbers, packed with herbs and spices, turned into tangy dill spears.

I treasure those memories and our family tradition. What's more, I still use those skills today. While there's something seemingly old-fashioned about what we Southerners call "putting up," preserving remains an integral part of any good Southern cook's repertoire. My family would preserve gallons at a time in all-day marathons, both at home and at community canning centers. That kind of volume and time commitment can be daunting for modern cooks and those who lack big gardens or the time to tend them. But, truth be told, anyone who can boil a pot of water can make a pickle. You don't need a truckload of produce for a small-batch jelly recipe. And refrigerator or freezer versions of pickles and preserves help even the busiest cooks enjoy putting up.

No matter the size of the batch, there's something amazingly satisfying about preserving food. I love the aroma of vinegar and warm spices and the impromptu steam facial I get while making pickles. Pushing a fingertip through a puddle of gemlike liquid on an ice-cold plate and seeing that your jelly is indeed, gelling, brings a joy like no other. I smile every time I hear the subtle pop of a lid dimpling down on a cooling jar, the telltale sign of a successful seal. To see colorful jars cooling on a windowsill—with the sun illuminating them like stained glass—is delicious in more ways than one.

More than that, putting up foods at the height of their freshness means you can have summer-ripe tomatoes in January and July-perfect peaches in February, and you don't have to muddle through winter with flavorless produce shipped from afar. Preserving can be economical too: Food is often least expensive when it is most plentiful and close at hand. And when you put up food yourself, you know where it comes from and exactly what's in the jar.

To be fair, canning is more than simply boiling water. Food science factors in when it comes to keeping good flavors in and bad microbes out. Most importantly, you need a reliable recipe and a bit of common sense. If you've picked up this book, you are well on your way to enjoying the sensual and practical pleasures of putting up. The recipes in this collection are based on recognized canning procedures, tested to perfection by kitchen professionals, and carefully written to address modern food safety concerns. They come with the seal of approval of *Southern Living*, one of the only magazines I wasn't allowed to cut up for paper dolls as a child. *Southern Living* recipes have been a delicious and trusted part of my life for as long as I can remember, combining established traditions with updated flavors and the casual ease that is a hallmark of life in the South.

This perfectly sized collection includes recipes for the shelf, the fridge, and the freezer, as well as recipes for the table to help you utilize the foods you've bottled and jarred. Small batches and step-by-step instructions are certain to lessen anxiety for newcomers to canning, and recipes with modern twists such as Cardamom-Plum Jam and Peanut-Washed Bourbon are ideal for those already bitten by the preserving bug.

There's even a putting-up party chapter from me (page 106) to get your friends and family in on the action—complete with menus, planning tips, and ideas for labeling and sharing little jars that are guaranteed to bring big smiles all year round.

◆

Bon appétit, y'all!

Virginia Willis

CANNING BASICS

1

A SHORT HISTORY OF HOME CANNING

❖

Whether you're new to canning or an old hand at putting up, it's comforting to know that people have been preserving food for millennia.

Long before there were glass jars to pack them in, there were pickled foods and potted jams. The term "canning" dates back to the military practice of putting food in tin canisters or "cans," the method that kept Napoleon's French soldiers fed in the early 1800s.

Glass jars weren't widely used in the United States for home food preservation until after the Civil War. Early American cooks preserved foods mostly by smoking or drying them—or by putting them in crocks with salt, vinegar, sugar, or alcohol solutions; keeping them in the root cellar; periodically scraping off surface molds and scum; and taking their chances.

Self-sealing heatproof Mason jars, named for the fellow who invented them, were developed in the 1850s, and early attempts at canning in them yielded more than a few exploding jars, food poisonings, and deaths. It wasn't until 1915 that scientists identified what was causing botulism poisoning, and the U.S. Department of Agriculture began developing guidelines to keep the anaerobic bacteria from canned goods. Modern canning practices—using heat, pressure, and acidity to kill or slow bacteria—stem from this.

Newer revelations about canning include:

• Those paraffin wax seals Grandma used on jams are a no-no. So is letting hot food cool in a hot jar to create a vacuum. Processing jars with canning lids in a covered pot of boiling water or a pressure canner for a specified length of time is essential.

• The acid or pH level of tomatoes and other foods can vary considerably depending on ripeness, freshness, variety, and growing conditions. Recipes that worked fine in the 1950s might not work as well with modern varieties and changing climates.

• Certain low-acid foods (meats, fish, most vegetables, ripe tomatoes, and some fruits) are most reliably and safely canned in a pressure canner. Alternatives include adding acid (vinegar or bottled lemon juice or citric acid powder) to the food before boiling-water canning—or preparing it for refrigerator or freezer storage rather than for the shelf.

• The density of the canned food (thin slices versus whole cucumbers) and the altitude where you're canning (11 feet above sea level in Mobile, Alabama, or 13,000 feet in Denver, Colorado) affect sterilization and processing time. The thicker the food and the higher the altitude, the longer you'll have to boil.

A LITTLE FOOD SCIENCE

There are three primary ways to halt or stop the growth of harmful bacteria that naturally occur in food: Heat or chill them to extremes, deprive them of oxygen and free water, and add enough acid to keep them from growing.

All three come into play in canning. To what degree and in what combination depend largely on how acidic the food is.

Acidity is measured in terms of pH. The higher the acidity, the lower the pH. On the scale (which ranges from 0 to 14, with 0 being the most acidic, 7 being neutral, and 14 being the most alkaline), 4.6 is the number to remember. It's the bacterial breaking point.

Foods with a pH of 4.6 or lower (such as lemons and other citrus fruits) are considered high-acid foods. They contain enough acid to knock down bacteria that survive boiling and vacuum sealing in jars in a boiling-water canner.

Foods with a pH above 4.6 (meat, seafood, many vegetables, certain fruits) are low-acid foods. In these foods, botulism can grow at room temperature even after boiling and vacuum sealing.

To keep botulism from rearing up inside the jar, these foods must have enough acid (vinegar or lemon juice or citric acid) added to them to bring the pH below 4.6 or be heated under pressure in a pressure canner to temperatures not achieved by mere boiling. Alternately, they may be acidified and stored for shorter periods in the refrigerator or the freezer.

BOOK METHODOLOGY

Preserving in small batches helps ensure quality and allows you to can a little bit of a lot of things year-round. It means you don't need an extra stove or a wheelbarrow full of produce to get started, and you likely won't put up more than you'll use in a year. That's what we focus on in this book.

The recipes that follow generally require less than one full grocery bag of produce and one timed session in the canning pot. Each makes four to eight half-pints, three to five pints, or two to three quarts. The selection includes tried-and-true recipes from *Southern Living* that have been scaled down for smaller yields, pH tested, and updated to include best canning practices based on guidelines and recipes from the National Center for Home Food Preservation at The University of Georgia, jarmaker Ball, and university extension services.

Most of our recipes involve boiling-water canning to make them shelf-stable for up to a year. (We didn't delve into pressure canning, which deserves its own book.) For safety, convenience, or the best flavor and texture, some recipes are designed for storage in the refrigerator or freezer rather than on the shelf.

"For the table" recipes included throughout provide unique ways to incorporate the items you've canned into your cooking. The yield with each recipe indicates how many and what size jars you'll need as well as where the final product is headed—the shelf, the fridge, the freezer, or the table.

little jars, big flavors

GETTING STARTED

❖

CHOOSING & WASHING PRODUCE

For canning, always choose firm, ripe, recently harvested produce. Avoid blemished and overripe fruits and vegetables. Opt for organic when the peels will be used—as in marmalades and whole preserves.

Wash produce gently under cold running water, scrubbing only if needed to remove waxy coatings. Trim roots, stems, and any blemished or bruised spots.

CHOOSING & WASHING JARS

Because canning jars of the same volume come in multiple shapes (slender half-pints can look almost as big as standard pints), it can be easy to confuse sizes. But jar size is critical to recipe success and safety. Look for markings on the bottom and sides of the jars, and use a measuring cup and water if you're not sure. Four-ounce jars hold a half cup. Half-pints hold one cup. Pints hold two cups. Quarts hold four cups. Standard and widemouthed jars can be used interchangeably, as long as they have the same volume. Widemouthed jars need widemouthed lids and bands.

Whether your jars are new or old, inspect them carefully. Discard any with chips, bubbles, and cracks, as they may break in the canner. Use bands that are free of rust. If your jars have mineral or hard water deposits from previous canning, soak them overnight in a vinegar solution (one cup vinegar for each gallon of water) to remove the cloudy film. Wash jars and bands in the dishwasher or in a basin of hot soapy water. Rinse thoroughly, and let air dry. Always use new lids.

GATHERING UP THE GEAR

Beyond the jars, bands, and lids, the basic canning gear (pages 18–19) may already be in your kitchen.

If you don't have a canning pot with a rack, you can use a large stockpot or Dutch oven with a lid, as long as the pot is wide enough to hold the number of jars called for in the recipe and three inches deeper than your rack and jars.

If you don't have a canning rack, you can use a round trivet or cooling rack that fits in the pot, or even a folded towel on top of a few jar bands, to keep jars off the bottom. This minimizes risk of jar breakage and allows boiling water to flow all around the jars.

Though a jar lifter with curved sides and rubberized grips is ideal for handling hot jars, regular tongs or a waterproof silicone oven mitt can be used in a pinch. And, while a candy thermometer is helpful for testing the readiness of jams and jellies, you can also figure it out with a cold saucer or a spoon (page 26).

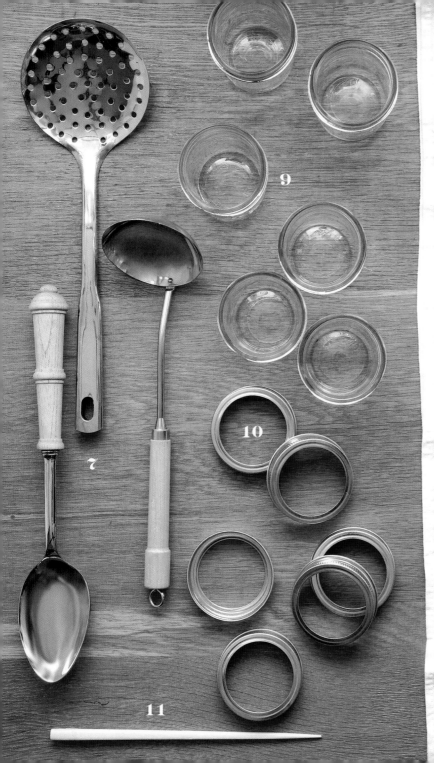

BASIC GEAR

1. CANNING POT large enough to hold rack, jars, and water to cover by 2 inches, and **A RACK** that holds jars off bottom **2. RUBBER-COATED JAR LIFTER** to maneuver jars in and out of the pot **3. TONGS** or lid wand to transfer lids from hot water to jars **4. STONEWARE BAKING DISH** or heatproof bowl for warming lids **5. WIDEMOUTHED FUNNEL** to keep jar rims clean **6. KITCHEN TIMER** to time the boil **7. NONREACTIVE SAUCEPAN** (enameled or stainless steel-clad metal, not aluminum), **MEASURING CUP** (glass is nice), and **UTENSILS** (wood or stainless steel spoon, ladle, and slotted spoon/skimmer) to avoid chemical reactions with brines and other acidic mixtures that can cause a metallic taste **8. NEW CANNING LIDS,** the flat metal discs with the rubbery ring seal on one side **9. NEW OR USED GLASS JARS** specifically designed for canning, such as Ball- or Kerr-brand Mason jars, as long as they are free of chips, bubbles, or cracks **10. NEW OR USED BANDS,** the screw-top rings that secure the lids until they are sealed **11. CHOPSTICK** or other small plastic, ceramic, or wooden tool to remove air bubbles **12. CLEAN TOWELS OR WOODEN CUTTING BOARD** on which to rest the hot jars and paper towels to wipe rims

INGREDIENTS NOT TO FUDGE

• **Vinegar:** Use vinegars labeled 5% acidity.

• **Lemon juice:** Bottled lemon juice has a more constant acidity than fresh lemon juice. In recipes that rely on lemon juice not just for flavor but for the proper acidity, such as those involving ripe tomatoes, we specify—and you should use—bottled lemon juice for safety.

• **Water for pickling brines:** Use soft or distilled water because minerals in hard water can cause discoloration (think: safe but unsightly blue garlic) and also unsafely lower the pH of pickled low-acid foods. (For instructions on softening hard water, see page 29.)

• **Canning-and-pickling salt:** Do not substitute kosher, sea, table, or other salts, which have different volumes and may contain additives that cloud brines.

• **Sugar:** Don't futz with the amount. If you decrease it in jam and jelly recipes, it may alter the sugar's ability to keep the food preserved once it's opened as well as reduce your odds of getting that jelly to set.

• **Pectin:** Some fruit preserves rely on the pectin naturally occurring in the fruit or its peels or seeds for thickening; others use a precanning fermentation or long cooking. If the recipe uses added pectin, be sure to use the type and amount specified. Powdered generally sets up firmer than liquid and thus is often preferred for jellies and marmalades. Liquid is often better suited to softer jams and looser preserves. And some are specifically designed for freezer preserves (sometimes labeled freezer, sometimes labeled instant).

METHODS NOT TO FUDGE

• **Boil times for sterilizing and processing:** These are key to safety. Set your timer only after the water has come or returned to a boil.

• **Warming method for lids:** The flexible compound that forms the seal needs only to be warmed in hot water to soften. Boiling lids before they go onto the jars can damage the seal. Also, be sure they're not clumped together in the warming bowl or pot. You want each one to get adequately softened but not to stick to its neighbor.

• **Jar size and headspace:** Processing times are based on the density of the food and the volume in the jar. If a jar is underfilled, not all of the air will be forced out during the process, and you won't get a good seal. If it's overfilled, the food can bubble out during processing and get stuck between the lid and the jar; there again, you won't get a good seal. And if you use the wrong-size jar, you may not be processing long enough.

• **Timing of steps so hot food goes into hot jars:** Jars need to be sterilized while you're finishing up the food that's going in them so that everything's hot when they meet. If your food prep ends up taking longer, just keep the jars in the pot at a low simmer until you're ready.

• **Transfering full jars:** Don't tip filled jars as you put them in or remove them from the water bath, which can sully the rim and interfere with the seal.

• **Checking the seals:** Always remove the bands and check lid seals 12 to 24 hours after canning. If jars aren't sealed, they're not safe to store on the shelf.

GENERAL INSTRUCTIONS
FOR BOILING-WATER CANNING

—◆—

STERILIZE JARS &
PREPARE LIDS

Place clean canning jars on a rack in the bottom of the canning pot, and add water to fill the jars and cover them by two inches **(1)**. Cover the pot, and bring the water to a rolling boil over high heat.

After the water reaches a boil, boil for 10 minutes, adjusting time as needed for your altitude*; then reduce the heat, and maintain at a simmer until you're ready to fill the jars. Jars must be hot when food or hot mixtures go into them.

Place the lids in a stoneware baking dish or heatproof bowl. Fan them out to ensure they're not clumped together.

FILL & PROCESS JARS

Remove jars from the simmering water using a jar lifter, and carefully pour the water in the jars back into the pot. Place the jars upright on a clean towel or large wooden cutting board. Ladle enough simmering water over the lids to cover them **(2)**. This warms the gasket on the underside of the lid and helps them seal. Cover the pot, and maintain at a simmer.

Pack any recipe-specified solid ingredients (such as herbs or cut vegetables for a pickle) into the hot jars. Ladle or pour hot mixture or brine into the hot jars, using a widemouthed funnel to help keep the jar rims clean **(3)**. Leave the recipe-specified amount of head-space, the space from the very top of the jar to the surface of the liquid or food inside **(4)**. Repeat with remaining jars, working quickly to ensure that hot mixtures go into hot jars.

Tap the jars lightly to help the contents settle, and stir gently with a chopstick or thin plastic or wooden utensil to free any trapped air bubbles **(5)**. Add more hot mixture or brine as needed to reach the correct headspace. Wipe the rims clean of any spilled food using a paper towel dipped in hot water.

Pour the water from the stoneware dish with the lids into the canning pot, and use tongs or a magnetic lid wand to quickly place a lid, white side down, on top of each jar.

Place a band onto each jar; screw just until fingertip-tight **(6)**. Do not overtighten. *(continued on page 25 »)*

*If you're canning at altitudes above 1,000 feet above sea level, you must adjust boiling times. If you're at 1,001 to 6,000 feet above sea level, add 5 minutes boiling time. If you're at altitudes of 6,001 feet or higher, add 10 minutes boiling time. You can find approximate elevations of land features in your area with the U.S. Geological Survey online tool (http://geonames.usgs.gov/pls/gnispublic). For the most accurate altitudes, check with your local government, planning commission, or cooperative extension service.

7

8

9

10

11

12

Carefully lower the filled jars into the pot of simmering water using the jar lifter to keep them upright **(7)**. Tipping can cause food to get between the jar and the lid and interfere with the seal. Add more water if needed to bring the water level to two inches above the jar tops.

Cover the pot, increase the heat, and return the water to a full rolling boil. After the water reaches a boil, set a timer, and boil for the amount of time specified in the recipe, adjusting if needed for your altitude **(8).***

Turn off the heat, uncover the pot, and wait until the boiling has subsided (about 5 minutes). Remove jars using the jar lifter, being careful to keep them upright **(7).**

Transfer jars to a towel-lined or wooden surface where they can rest undisturbed 12 to 24 hours **(9)**. Do not tighten or adjust bands. Lids may make a popping noise as the jars cool. Not to worry. That's one sign of an airtight seal—and the sound of canning success.

CHECK SEALS, LABEL & STORE

When the jars have cooled 12 to 24 hours, remove the bands and inspect the lids. Each lid should be sucked down a little in the middle and firmly attached at the edges. Press down on the center of each lid with your finger **(10)**. If the lid doesn't move, the jar is sealed and can be stored in a cool, dark place for up to 1 year (or as specified in the recipe).

If the lid center depresses and pops up again, the jar isn't sealed and should be refrigerated immediately and its contents used within a few days. (You can reheat the contents of an improperly sealed jar, pack in a freshly sterilized hot jar, and process again, though this can alter the desired texture and flavor.)

Label and store properly sealed jars without the bands **(11)**. This allows you to better spot oozing, surface mold, rusting, and other signs of spoilage around the lid and frees up the bands for another canning batch. Refrigerate jars after opening.

WHAT TO DO WITH PARTIAL JARS

Depending on how fast you simmered, how much you skimmed off when removing foam, how much you tasted along the way, and the quality of your produce, you may have a few tablespoons more or less than you need for the proper headspace. Tempting though it may be, don't overfill the jars, and don't process jars that are only partially full **(12)**. Headspace is critical to achieving an airtight seal and proper processing. Too little headspace and your mixture may boil over during processing and get between the lid and the jar. Too much and it may overcook and never force out enough air to produce a vacuum seal. Instead, enjoy any partial jars immediately, or refrigerate and use within a week.

*If you're canning at altitudes above 1,000 feet above sea level, you must adjust boiling times. If you're at 1,001 to 6,000 feet above sea level, add 5 minutes boiling time. If you're at altitudes of 6,001 feet or higher, add 10 minutes boiling time. You can find approximate elevations of land features in your area with the U.S. Geological Survey online tool (http://geonames.usgs.gov/pls/gnispublic). For the most accurate altitudes, check with your local government, planning commission, or cooperative extension service.

GEL TESTS FOR JAMS, JELLIES & PRESERVES

◆

Use these tests to check for thickening when your fruit mixture begins to sputter more than foam, and the surface takes on a glossy sheen.

TEMP TEST

Use a candy thermometer while the mixture boils or simmers. Remove from the heat when the mixture registers 220°, the temperature at which fruit-sugar mixtures gel.

FREEZER TEST

Put a few saucers in the freezer to chill before you cook the fruit mixture. When it appears to have thickened or hits the cook time specified in the recipe, spoon a small amount onto a chilled saucer. Wait a few seconds then push a trail through it with your finger. Does it wrinkle at the edge, form a slight skin, and hold the trail? It's likely set. Does it part briefly and then run back together like honey? Cook it a bit more, and repeat the test.

DRIP TEST

Run a spoon through the jelly or jam, and turn the spoon on its side, letting the mixture run off the spoon. Does it drip rapidly in individual drops? It's not set. Do the last drops combine and lazily fall in a sheet from the back of the spoon? It's likely set.

HELPFUL HINTS
FROM THE THE TEST KITCHEN

‹ ◆ ›

☐ Start with hot water in the canning pot to reduce the time it takes to come to a boil.

☐ If you don't have soft water and are using hard water to sterilize and process jars, add ¼ cup vinegar for each gallon of water in the canning pot to avoid leaving cloudy mineral deposits on the jars.

☐ Always use new canning lids purchased within the past year. Even if the package is unopened and the lids are unused, the seals can degrade over time.

☐ Save the boxes that canning jars are sold in; they come in handy when transporting canned products and storing the emptied jars for reuse.

☐ Use a Microplane to zest citrus. It produces tiny strands that are uniform in the final product and avoids pith that can turn canned goods bitter or cloudy.

☐ If the spices and herbs you're using aren't going in the finished jar, put them in cheesecloth tied with kitchen string to make them easier to fish out. You don't want to be hunting for a rosemary sprig in a pot of scalding hot jam.

☐ Use the size of saucepan or Dutch oven specified in the recipe, even if it seems larger at first than you think you need. Larger pans help avoid boilover.

☐ A small stoneware baking dish is ideal for warming lids. It holds heat nicely, is wide enough to let you scatter the lids and keep them from sticking together, and is shallow enough to make fishing out the lids easy.

☐ Don't stir jam or jelly mixtures with whisks. That can introduce air bubbles you don't want in the finished product. Use a wooden or nonaluminum spoon.

☐ Jam- and jelly-making can be sticky business. You'll be stirring often. Have a clean spoon rest handy to minimize sticky stove-tops and counters and avoid introducing counter bacteria into your fruit mixture.

☐ Always let boiled mixtures stand off the heat at least one minute before skimming. This allows the foam to rise and the food to settle, making skimming easier.

☐ Stir mixtures after skimming and before and between ladling into jars to ensure each jar gets an equal amount of mixed solids or liquid and solids.

☐ Fill jars on wax paper-lined jelly-roll pans to catch drips and make moving the jars from your workspace to the stove easier.

☐ Many preserves with added spices and herbs—and most canned pickles—taste best and achieve their best texture after three weeks in the jar.

little jars, big flavors

☐ Having doubts about your jelly setting after you've canned it? Look at what's left in the pot. Does it cling to the sides? It's likely set. If your jelly or jam seems too thin when you check the seals, don't fret. Some jellies take a week or more to fully set. If yours doesn't after two weeks, call it syrup, and store it in the fridge. It'll still taste great.

☐ Using soft or distilled water (as opposed to hard water) when canning helps prevent unintended chemical reactions between minerals in the water and items in the jar.

☐ If you have hard water (you'll know if it leaves rust or calcium deposits on your faucets and fixtures), you can soften it by boiling it for 15 minutes, letting it stand 24 hours, and pouring off carefully to leave settled sediment at the bottom.

☐ Screw-top freezer-safe plastic containers are good options for freezer preserves.

☐ If you freeze preserves in glass jars, be sure to thaw the frozen jars one day in the fridge before using. Don't run a frozen jar under hot water or put it in the microwave. Frozen glass jars may crack with a severe temperature change.

☐ Though pretty, antique jars and used one-piece lids are not safe for boiling-water canners. Save them for refrigerator versions and items you keep in the fridge or bring to the table.

☐ Always use a new lid, a rust-free band, and a jar free of chips, cracks, and bubbles that is specifically made for canning if you're going to put it in the canning pot.

SPOILAGE SIGNS TO WATCH FOR

• Foaming or fizzing in the jar after it's been sealed

• Rancid, sour, or yeasty odors when you open the jar

• Food bubbling in or exploding from a sealed jar

• Lids that bulge or loosen after initial sealing

• Powder, mold, or film on the surface of the food

NOT IDEAL, BUT USUALLY NOT A BIG DEAL

• Cloudiness in the jar if you've used ground spices or table salt in the recipe. Those ingredients can cloud a brine.

• Film on the outside of the jar. Most often this is just a hard water or mineral deposit from the water in your canner.

• Black specks on the bottom of the lids of canned tomatoes. It's a natural reaction and doesn't alone signal spoilage.

• Blue garlic at the bottom of your pickles. If garlic's very young, not fully dried out, or not completely cooked, a component in it may react with copper in your cookware or minerals in your water, making it turn blue. It's unsightly but not harmful.

• Fruit float. If the fruit pieces in your preserves float to the top of the jar rather than being suspended evenly throughout, it's OK. That jar probably won't win you a blue ribbon at the fair, but it'll still be delicious. Just give the contents a stir when you open the jar.

• When in doubt, throw it out!

JAMS, JELLIES & SPREADS

2

If you've never made jam before, here's a good place to start. This one comes together quickly, requires no pectin, and bursts with ripe berry flavor. The combination of three berries gives the jam a rich hue and a hauntingly wild, sweet-tart flavor.

MIXED BERRY JAM

2 (6-oz.) packages fresh blackberries (2½ cups)
1 (6-oz.) container fresh raspberries (1½ cups)
1 pt. fresh blueberries (2 cups)
3 cups sugar
1 Tbsp. fresh lime juice

makes: 4 (½-pt.) jars for the shelf

hands-on time: 40 min.

total time: 50 min., plus 1 week standing time

1. Rinse berries thoroughly under cold running water. Remove and discard stems and any blemished berries. Mash with a potato masher until evenly crushed.

2. Sterilize jars, and prepare lids as described on page 22.

3. While jars are boiling, bring crushed berries and sugar to a rolling boil in an 8-qt. stainless steel or enameled Dutch oven over medium-high heat, stirring occasionally, until sugar dissolves. Boil, stirring often, 7 minutes or until a candy thermometer registers 220°. Remove from heat, and let foam settle (about 1 minute). Skim off and discard any foam.

4. Fill, seal, and process jars as described on pages 22–25, leaving ¼-inch headspace and processing 5 minutes.

5. Remove jars from water, and let stand, undisturbed, at room temperature 24 hours. To check seals, remove the bands, and press down on the center of each lid. If the lid doesn't move, the jar is sealed. If the lid depresses and pops up again, the jar is not sealed. Store properly sealed jars in a cool, dark place up to 1 year. Refrigerate after opening.

NOTE: If you prefer a seedless jam, heat the crushed berries without sugar until they are soft. Press them through a sieve or a food mill. Add sugar, and proceed as directed.

little jars, big flavors

This lickety-split jam is a great way to use up extra blueberries. You'll have it sealed in jars and cooling on the windowsill in less than an hour. Though you can use it sooner, it achieves its ideal texture about three weeks after canning.

BLUEBERRY-LEMON JAM

3	cups fresh blueberries	1	Tbsp. fresh lemon juice
3½	cups sugar	1	(3-oz.) package liquid pectin
1	tsp. finely grated lemon zest		

1. Sterilize jars, and prepare lids as described on page 22.

2. While jars are boiling, wash, drain, and lightly crush blueberries with a spoon (just enough to split the skins). Measure 2½ cups crushed blueberries into a 6-qt. stainless steel or enameled Dutch oven. Stir in sugar and next 2 ingredients. Bring to a rolling boil, stirring occasionally. Boil 1 minute, stirring constantly. Remove from heat, and immediately stir in pectin. Let foam settle (about 1 minute). Skim off and discard any foam.

3. Fill, seal, and process jars as described on pages 22–25, leaving ¼-inch headspace and processing 10 minutes.

4. Remove jars from water, and let stand, undisturbed, at room temperature 24 hours. To check seals, remove the bands, and press down on the center of each lid. If the lid doesn't move, the jar is sealed. If the lid depresses and pops up again, the jar is not sealed. Store properly sealed jars in a cool, dark place up to 1 year. Refrigerate after opening.

Cardamom lends pizzazz to this jam, which is delicious with roast pork or duck, or on biscuits or scones. Because plums have variable pectin levels, it may take a few minutes more or less to get to the syrupy stage. Just keep boiling and stirring, and let your thermometer be your guide.

CARDAMOM-PLUM JAM

4   lb. black plums, pitted and chopped (10 cups)

2   cups sugar

3   Tbsp. fresh lime juice

1½   tsp. ground cardamom

1. Bring plums and sugar to a boil in an 8-qt. stainless steel or enameled Dutch oven over medium-high heat, stirring often. Reduce heat, and simmer 5 minutes or until plums soften, stirring often. Pour mixture through a colander into a bowl, using back of a spoon to squeeze out juice to measure 4½ cups. Reserve 2 cups pulp.

2. Sterilize jars, and prepare lids as described on page 22.

3. While jars are boiling, pour reserved 4½ cups plum juice into Dutch oven; bring to a boil over medium-high heat, stirring occasionally. Boil, stirring occasionally, 15 to 17 minutes or until syrupy and a candy thermometer registers 220°. Stir in reserved 2 cups plum pulp and any accumulated juices. Stir in lime juice and cardamom. Bring to a boil over medium-high heat, stirring often. Reduce heat, and simmer, stirring constantly, 5 minutes or until very thick. Remove from heat; let foam settle (about 1 minute). Skim off and discard any foam.

4. Fill, seal, and process jars as described on pages 22–25, leaving ¼-inch headspace and processing 5 minutes.

5. Remove jars from water, and let stand, undisturbed, at room temperature 24 hours. To check seals, remove the bands, and press down on the center of each lid. If the lid doesn't move, the jar is sealed. If the lid depresses and pops up again, the jar is not sealed. Store properly sealed jars in a cool, dark place up to 1 year. Refrigerate after opening.

makes: 5 (½-pt.) jars for the shelf

hands-on time: 1 hour

total time: 1 hour, 10 min., plus 1 week standing time

NOTE: If plums are firm and pits do not pull away easily, you can cut the pits out. Place plum on a cutting board. Slice off rounded sides, cutting close to the pit. Lay section with pit on board, and slice off plum portion from top and bottom. Discard the small cube containing the pit.

little jars, big flavors

This pretty jam captures the bright flavor of two of spring's earliest fruits: tart rhubarb and sweet strawberries.

STRAWBERRY-RHUBARB JAM

4½ cups (¼-inch-thick) sliced fresh rhubarb
½ cup fresh orange juice
1 qt. ripe fresh strawberries
5½ cups sugar
1 (3-oz.) package liquid pectin

1. Combine rhubarb and orange juice in a 3-qt. stainless steel saucepan. Cover and bring to a boil over medium-high heat. Uncover, reduce heat, and simmer, stirring often, 5 minutes or until rhubarb is tender.

2. Wash strawberries; remove and discard stems and hulls. Mash strawberries with a potato masher until evenly crushed.

3. Sterilize jars, and prepare lids as described on page 22.

4. While jars are boiling, measure 2 cups cooked rhubarb and 1¾ cups mashed strawberries into a 6-qt. stainless steel or enameled Dutch oven. Stir in sugar. Bring to a rolling boil over high heat, stirring constantly. Whisk in pectin. Return to a rolling boil, and boil hard 1 minute. Remove from heat, and let foam settle (about 1 minute). Skim off and discard any foam.

5. Fill, seal, and process jars as described on pages 22–25, leaving ¼-inch headspace and processing 10 minutes.

6. Remove jars from water, and let stand, undisturbed, at room temperature 24 hours. To check seals, remove the bands, and press down on the center of each lid. If the lid doesn't move, the jar is sealed. If the lid depresses and pops up again, the jar is not sealed. Store properly sealed jars in a cool, dark place up to 1 year. Refrigerate after opening.

makes: 8 (½-pt.) jars
for the shelf

hands-on time: 40 min.

total time: 55 min.,
plus 1 week standing time

Basil plays a subtle role in this sparkling pink-red jam, elevating but not overwhelming the star: strawberries. Bruising the basil leaves with the back of a knife helps release their essential oils and flavor. Tucking the leaves in cheesecloth makes them easier to fish out of the hot fruit mixture.

STRAWBERRY-BASIL JAM

2   lb. fresh strawberries
2½ cups sugar
2   Tbsp. fresh lemon juice
1   cup packed fresh basil leaves,
    washed, dried, bruised slightly,
    and tied in cheesecloth

1   (1¾-oz.) package powdered
    pectin

makes: 5 (½-pt.) jars
for the shelf

hands-on time: 40 min.

total time: 55 min., plus 1 week
standing time

1. Sterilize jars, and prepare lids as described on page 22.

2. While jars are boiling, wash and hull strawberries. Mash berries in a 6-qt. stainless steel or enameled Dutch oven with a potato masher until evenly crushed. Add sugar and next 2 ingredients. Bring to a rolling boil over high heat. Boil, stirring often, 10 minutes. Remove basil and cheesecloth.

3. Sprinkle pectin over strawberry mixture, and stir well. Return to a rolling boil. Boil 1 minute. Remove from heat, and let foam settle (about 1 minute). Skim off and discard any foam.

4. Fill, seal, and process jars as described on pages 22–25, leaving ¼-inch headspace and processing 10 minutes.

5. Remove jars from water, and let stand, undisturbed, at room temperature 24 hours. To check seals, remove the bands, and press down on the center of each lid. If the lid doesn't move, the jar is sealed. If the lid depresses and pops up again, the jar is not sealed. Store properly sealed jars in a cool, dark place up to 1 year. Refrigerate after opening.

little jars, big flavors

This jam gets a brilliant ruby color and intense flavor from a not-so-secret ingredient: ruby port. Use it as a filling or topping and add boozy indulgence to everything from layer cakes and thumbprint cookies to sweet potato biscuits and baked Brie. Or try it in place of cranberry sauce, and serve it with Thanksgiving turkey or Christmas goose.

STRAWBERRY-PORT JAM

2	1b. fresh strawberries	1	(1¾-oz.) package powdered pectin
1½	cups ruby port	4	cups sugar
1	tsp. lemon zest		
½	tsp. ground nutmeg		

1. Sterilize jars, and prepare lids as described on page 22.

2. While jars are boiling, wash strawberries, remove and discard stems and hulls, and chop. Mash with a potato masher until evenly crushed.

3. Measure 3⅓ cups crushed strawberries into a 6-qt. stainless steel or enameled Dutch oven. Stir in ruby port and next 3 ingredients. Bring mixture to a full rolling boil, and boil, stirring constantly, 1 minute. Add sugar, stirring constantly, and return to a rolling boil. Boil 1 minute. Remove from heat, and let foam settle (about 1 minute). Skim off and discard any foam.

4. Fill, seal, and process jars as described on pages 22–25, leaving ¼-inch headspace and processing 10 minutes.

5. Remove jars from water, and let stand, undisturbed, at room temperature 24 hours. To check seals, remove the bands, and press down on the center of each lid. If the lid doesn't move, the jar is sealed. If the lid depresses and pops up again, the jar is not sealed. Store properly sealed jars in a cool, dark place up to 1 year. Refrigerate after opening.

makes: 6 (½-pt.) jars
for the shelf

hands-on time: 40 min.

total time: 55 min.,
plus 1 week standing time

NOTE: Ruby port is a deep red sweet wine aged in wood and typically enjoyed as an after-dinner drink. Because it can have a higher alcohol content than other wines, it's sometimes stocked with the hard liquor rather than the wines.

Spiked with bourbon and ginger, this pretty-as-a-Chilton-County-peach jam oozes Southern comfort. You don't need all that many peaches to get nine jars, which makes this a particularly good jam for gifts.

PEACH-BOURBON JAM

4	lb. peaches	2	Tbsp. finely chopped	
7	cups sugar		crystallized ginger	
¼	cup lemon juice	1	(3-oz.) package liquid pectin	
¼	cup bourbon			

1. Sterilize jars, and prepare lids as described on page 22.

2. While jars are boiling, peel peaches with a vegetable peeler, pit, and coarsely chop. Measure 4½ cups chopped peaches into a 6-qt. stainless steel or enameled Dutch oven, and mash with a potato masher until evenly crushed. Stir in sugar and next 3 ingredients.

3. Bring mixture to a rolling boil; boil 1 minute, stirring constantly. Remove from heat. Stir in pectin. Let foam settle (about 1 minute). Skim off and discard any foam.

4. Fill, seal, and process jars as described on pages 22–25, leaving ¼-inch headspace and processing 5 minutes.

5. Remove jars from water, and let stand, undisturbed, at room temperature 24 hours. To check seals, remove the bands, and press down on the center of each lid. If the lid doesn't move, the jar is sealed. If the lid depresses and pops up again, the jar is not sealed. Store properly sealed jars in a cool, dark place up to 1 year. Refrigerate after opening.

makes: 9 (½-pt.) jars
for the shelf

hands-on time: 35 min.

total time: 55 min.,
plus 1 week standing time

Boozy peach jam nestles between the creamy filling and the crumb crust for a delicious twist on the classic cheesecake. Be sure to include this recipe with the jar if you're giving the Peach-Bourbon Jam as a gift.

PEACH-BOURBON CHEESECAKE

1	cup graham cracker crumbs	2	Tbsp. bourbon
3	Tbsp. butter, melted	1	tsp. almond extract
1	cup plus 2 Tbsp. sugar, divided	1¼	cups sour cream, divided
3	Tbsp. all-purpose flour	4	large eggs
4	(8-oz.) packages cream cheese, softened	½	cup plus 2 Tbsp. Peach-Bourbon Jam (page 45), divided

makes: 10 to 12 servings for the table

hands-on time: 15 min.

total time: 5 hours, plus 1 day for chilling

1. Preheat oven to 325°. Stir together graham cracker crumbs, butter, and 2 Tbsp. sugar until crumbs are moistened; press mixture on bottom of a lightly greased 9-inch springform pan. Bake at 325° for 10 minutes. Cool on a wire rack. Reduce oven temperature to 300°.

2. Beat 1 cup sugar, flour, and cream cheese at medium speed with an electric mixer until smooth. Add bourbon and almond extract, beating just until blended. Add ¾ cup sour cream, beating just until blended. Add eggs, 1 at a time, beating at low speed just until blended after each addition. (Do not overbeat.)

3. Dot crust with spoonfuls of ½ cup of the jam. (Do not spread.) Pour batter over jam. Bake at 300° for 1 hour, 45 minutes or until cheesecake center barely moves when pan is touched. Turn oven off. Remove cheesecake; run a knife around outside edge of cheesecake to loosen from pan. Return cheesecake to oven, and partially open oven door. Cool cheesecake 1 hour in oven. Remove from oven; cool completely on a wire rack (2 hours). Cover and chill 8 to 24 hours.

4. Remove sides of pan. Spread remaining ½ cup sour cream over top of cheesecake; spoon remaining 2 Tbsp. jam in center of sour cream.

Rosemary and lime take peaches for a magical turn in this jam. Try it as a sauce for bacon-wrapped shrimp, a topping for soft cheeses, or as the glaze and sauce for our Peach-Rosemary Pork Tenderloin (page 50).

PEACH-ROSEMARY JAM

2½ lb. fresh peaches (5 large)
1 tsp. lime zest
¼ cup fresh lime juice
1 (1¾-oz.) package powdered
   pectin

2 (4-inch) rosemary sprigs
5 cups sugar

makes: 7 (½-pt.) jars
for the shelf

hands-on time: 55 min.

total time: 1 hour, 10 min.,
plus 1 week standing time

1. Sterilize jars, and prepare lids as described on page 22.

2. While jars are boiling, peel peaches with a vegetable peeler. Remove pits, and coarsely chop. Mash with a potato masher until evenly crushed. Measure 4 cups crushed peaches into a 6-qt. stainless steel or enameled Dutch oven. Stir in lime zest and next 3 ingredients, and bring to a rolling boil over medium-high heat, stirring often. Boil 1 minute, stirring constantly. Add sugar, and return to a rolling boil; boil 1 minute, stirring constantly. Remove from heat; discard rosemary. Let foam settle (about 1 minute). Skim off and discard any foam.

3. Fill, seal, and process jars as described on pages 22–25, leaving ¼-inch headspace and processing 5 minutes.

4. Remove jars from water, and let stand, undisturbed, at room temperature 24 hours. To check seals, remove the bands, and press down on the center of each lid. If the lid doesn't move, the jar is sealed. If the lid depresses and pops up again, the jar is not sealed. Store properly sealed jars in a cool, dark place up to 1 year. Refrigerate after opening.

Dijon mustard and garlic turn your homemade Peach-Rosemary Jam into the perfect accompaniment for that supper staple, the pork tenderloin.

PEACH-ROSEMARY PORK TENDERLOIN

makes: 4 servings
for the table

hands-on time: 10 min.

total time: 40 min.

2	tsp. canola oil		2	tsp. Dijon mustard
1	lb. pork tenderloin, trimmed		1	tsp. lemon zest
¼	tsp. salt		2	garlic cloves, minced
¼	tsp. freshly ground pepper			
½	cup Peach-Rosemary Jam (page 49)			

1. Preheat oven to 425°. Heat oil in a large cast-iron skillet over medium-high heat. Sprinkle pork with salt and pepper. Add pork to skillet; cook 4 minutes, turning to brown on all sides.

2. Combine jam and next 3 ingredients in a small saucepan. Cook over medium heat, stirring constantly, 1 minute or until jam melts. Set aside half of jam mixture for serving; set aside other half for basting. Brush 2 Tbsp. basting mixture over pork.

3. Bake, uncovered, at 425° for 13 to 15 minutes or until a meat thermometer inserted in center registers 145°, brushing with remaining 2 Tbsp. basting mixture after 5 minutes. Let pork stand 5 minutes before slicing. Serve with reserved jam mixture.

This jam makes just enough to share with your two best friends and still keep a little for yourself. Because of its long simmering, it's ideal to make while you're doing something else in or near the kitchen. Enjoy it at room temperature over grilled meats and fish or with cream cheese and crackers.

TOMATO-GINGER REFRIGERATOR JAM WITH LEMON VERBENA

5	lb. firm, ripe tomatoes	⅓	cup chopped garlic (10 cloves)
1½	cups sugar	⅓	cup minced fresh ginger
¾	cup fresh lime juice (4 medium)	1	(6-inch) lemon verbena sprig

makes: 3 (½-pt.) jars for the fridge

hands-on time: 2 hours

total time: 3 hours

1. Wash tomatoes. Cut an X in bottom of each tomato. Place tomatoes in a large pot of boiling water 30 seconds or until peel begins to separate from tomato flesh. Remove with a slotted spoon. Plunge into ice water to stop the cooking process; drain. Peel back skin using a paring knife, and discard.

2. Place a fine wire-mesh strainer over a bowl. Cut tomatoes in half crosswise, and squeeze gently to remove seeds, holding tomatoes over strainer to collect juices to measure 1 cup. Discard seeds, and trim off stem ends. Coarsely chop tomato halves to measure 6 cups.

3. Bring reserved 1 cup tomato juice, 6 cups coarsely chopped tomato, sugar, and remaining ingredients to a rolling boil in a 6-qt. stainless steel or enameled Dutch oven over medium-high heat. Reduce heat to medium-low, and simmer 5 minutes. Remove and discard lemon verbena sprig. Simmer, uncovered, stirring often, 1 hour or until mixture is thickened. (Keep a close eye on it near the end of the cooking, being careful not to let the bottom scorch.)

4. Spoon into clean canning jars or other heatproof, nonreactive containers with lids. Let cool 1 hour. Cover and chill. Store in refrigerator up to 3 weeks.

NOTE: Lemon verbena is an herb with an intense lemon aroma, making it a favorite of bees and butterflies. Look for sprigs (or whole plants for your garden) at farmers' markets, specialty grocers, and nurseries.

little jars, big flavors

53

Scuppernongs are a bronze variety of the sweet and fragrant thick-skinned muscadine grapes that grow in parts of the South in early fall. They can vary in size and juiciness from year to year. If yours yield less than 3⅔ cups juice, use 1½ cups sugar for every 1 cup of juice in step 4.

SCUPPERNONG JELLY

makes: 7 (½-pt.) jars
for the shelf

————

hands-on time: 1 hour, 5 min.

————

total time: 2 hours, 5 min.,
plus 1 week standing time

4	(1-qt.) packages ripe bronze Scuppernong grapes (about 5¼ lb.)
	Cheesecloth
5½	cups sugar
2	Tbsp. fresh lemon juice
1	(3-oz.) package liquid pectin

1. Wash Scuppernongs; remove and discard stems. Bring Scuppernongs and 1 cup water to a rolling boil in a 6-qt. stainless steel or enameled Dutch oven over medium-high heat, stirring often. Boil, stirring often, 20 minutes or until most of seeds have been released from pulp. Mash Scuppernongs with a potato masher to slip skins from pulp.

2. Line a large wire-mesh strainer with 3 layers of damp cheesecloth. Place over a large bowl. Pour Scuppernong mixture into strainer, and let drain at least 1 hour to measure 3⅔ cups juice. Discard solids.

3. Sterilize jars, and prepare lids as described on page 22.

4. While jars are boiling, pour reserved 3⅔ cups Scuppernong juice into Dutch oven. Stir in sugar and lemon juice. Bring to a rolling boil over medium-high heat, stirring constantly. Add pectin, and return to a rolling boil. Boil 1 minute. Remove from heat; let foam settle (about 1 minute). Skim off and discard any foam.

5. Fill, seal, and process jars as described on pages 22–25, leaving ¼-inch headspace and processing 5 minutes.

6. Remove jars from water, and let stand, undisturbed, at room temperature 24 hours. To check seals, remove the bands, and press down on the center of each lid. If the lid doesn't move, the jar is sealed. If the lid depresses and pops up again, the jar is not sealed. Store properly sealed jars in a cool, dark place up to 1 year. Refrigerate after opening.

Cinnamon, vanilla, and star anise add aroma and interest to the standard plum jelly. Layer it with peanut butter on toast for an ooey, gooey, grown-up PB and J.

SPICED PLUM JELLY

4¼ lb. fresh plums

4 star anise

4 (3-inch) cinnamon sticks

Cheesecloth

2 vanilla beans

1 (1¾-oz.) package powdered pectin

2¼ cups sugar

makes: 3 (½-pt.) jars
for the shelf

hands-on time: 20 min.

total time: 1 hour, 30 min.,
plus 1 week standing time

1. Wash plums. Cut plums in quarters, and remove pits. Place plums in an 8-qt. stainless steel or enameled Dutch oven; crush plums with a potato masher. Add 2 cups water, star anise, and cinnamon sticks. Bring to a boil; cover, reduce heat, and simmer 20 minutes or until fruit is soft.

2. Line a wire-mesh strainer with 2 layers of damp cheesecloth or a jelly bag. Place over a bowl. Pour plum mixture into srainer, and let drain 30 minutes or as needed to extract 3 cups juice. (Do not press or squeeze mixture.) Discard solids.

3. Sterilize jars, and prepare lids as described on page 22.

4. While jars are boiling, cut vanilla beans in half lengthwise. Scrape out and reserve seeds. Set aside vanilla bean pods for another use (such as Bottomless Vanilla Extract, page 221). Stir together 3 cups juice, vanilla bean seeds, and pectin in clean 8-qt. Dutch oven. Cook over high heat, stirring constantly, until mixture comes to a rolling boil. Stir in sugar; return to a rolling boil. Boil hard exactly 1 minute, stirring constantly. Remove from heat, and let foam settle (about 1 minute). Skim off and discard any foam.

5. Fill, seal, and process jars as described on pages 22–25, leaving ¼-inch headspace and processing 10 minutes.

6. Remove jars from water, and let stand, undisturbed, at room temperature 24 hours. To check seals, remove the bands, and press down on the center of each lid. If the lid doesn't move, the jar is sealed. If the lid depresses and pops up again, the jar is not sealed. Store properly sealed jars in a cool, dark place up to 1 year. Refrigerate after opening.

This jewel-colored jam starts with already squeezed juice, making it as quick and easy as it is perky.

POMEGRANATE-CHERRY JELLY

3½ cups bottled pomegranate-cherry juice

1 Tbsp. orange zest

1 (1¾-oz.) package powdered pectin

5 cups sugar

1. Sterilize jars, and prepare lids as described on page 22.

2. While jars are boiling, combine juice and orange zest in a 6-qt. stainless steel or enameled Dutch oven. Whisk in pectin until dissolved. Bring to a rolling boil over high heat, stirring often. Add sugar, stirring constantly, and return to a rolling boil. Boil, stirring constantly, 1 minute. Remove from heat, and let foam settle (about 1 minute). Skim off and discard any foam.

3. Fill, seal, and process jars as described on pages 22–25, leaving ¼-inch headspace and processing 10 minutes.

4. Remove jars from water, and let stand, undisturbed, at room temperature 24 hours. To check seals, remove the bands, and press down on the center of each lid. If the lid doesn't move, the jar is sealed. If the lid depresses and pops up again, the jar is not sealed. Store properly sealed jars in a cool, dark place up to 1 year. Refrigerate after opening.

makes: 6 (½-pt.) jars for the shelf

hands-on time: 10 min.

total time: 30 min., plus 1 week standing time

Try this over cream cheese with crackers or whisked into the Jalapeño Vinaigrette (next page).

JALAPEÑO JELLY

½ cup seeded and coarsely
  chopped jalapeño peppers (3 medium)
½ cup coarsely chopped green bell pepper
3 cups sugar
½ cup cider vinegar (5% acidity)
2 Tbsp. fresh lime juice
1 (3-oz.) package liquid pectin

1. Process peppers in a food processor 1 minute or until almost smooth, stopping to scrape down sides.

2. Bring pepper mixture, sugar, and vinegar to a rolling boil in a 4-qt. stainless steel or enameled Dutch oven over medium-high heat, stirring constantly. Boil 3 minutes, stirring occasionally. Stir in lime juice and pectin, and return to a rolling boil. Boil 1 minute, stirring constantly. Remove from heat, and let foam settle (about 1 minute). Skim off and discard any foam.

3. Spoon into clean canning jars or other heatproof, nonreactive containers with lids. Let cool 1 hour. Cover and chill. Store in refrigerator up to 3 weeks.

makes: 3 (½-pt.) jars
for the fridge

hands-on time: 30 min.

total time: 1 hour, 30 min.,
plus 1 day standing time

Drizzle this vinaigrette over a summer salad of chopped watermelon and heirloom tomatoes, sliced red onion, and fresh cilantro.

JALAPEÑO VINAIGRETTE

¼   cup Jalapeño Jelly (previous page)
3   Tbsp. white wine vinegar
2   Tbsp. fresh lime juice (1 large)
½   tsp. salt
¼   tsp. freshly ground pepper
1   garlic clove, minced
⅓   cup olive oil

1. Whisk together first 6 ingredients in a bowl. Gradually add oil in a slow, steady stream, whisking until blended. Store in refrigerator up to 1 week.

makes: about 1 cup
for the table

hands-on time: 8 min.

total time: 8 min.

TART
BASIL

These festive jellies make great Christmas presents. Their summery flavors work with sweet and savory dishes. The mint version goes nicely with goat cheese and roasted lamb—or with cream cheese and crackers if you're feeling a little less fancy. Try the tart basil version in place of mayonnaise on a BLT, as a glaze for seared chicken or shrimp, or spread on pound cake layered with sliced strawberries for an herb-spiked twist on shortcake.

MINT OR TART BASIL JELLY

6¼ cups sugar
1   cup loosely packed fresh mint
    leaves or 1½ cups loosely packed
    fresh basil leaves, rinsed,
    dried, bruised slightly, and tied
    in cheesecloth
1   cup white vinegar (5% acidity)
6   drops green liquid food coloring
2   (3-oz.) packages liquid pectin

1. Sterilize jars, and prepare lids as described on page 22.

2. While jars are boiling, bring 2 cups water, sugar, and next 3 ingredients to a rolling boil in a 6-qt. stainless steel or enameled Dutch oven. Add pectin, and return to a rolling boil. Boil 1 minute. Remove from heat; discard mint and cheesecloth. Let foam settle (about 1 minute). Skim off and discard any foam.

3. Fill, seal, and process jars as described on pages 22–25, leaving ¼-inch headspace and processing 5 minutes.

4. Remove jars from water, and let stand, undisturbed, at room temperature 24 hours. To check seals, remove the bands, and press down on the center of each lid. If the lid doesn't move, the jar is sealed. If the lid depresses and pops up again, the jar is not sealed. Store properly sealed jars in a cool, dark place up to 1 year. Refrigerate after opening.

makes: 7 (½-pt.) jars
for the shelf

hands-on time: 30 min.

total time: 45 min.,
plus 3 weeks standing time

NOTE: If yours looks more like Kool-Aid after canning, be patient. It can take up to three weeks to fully set.

Smooth a little of this peppery fruit spread on a cracker with your favorite creamy cheese. Brush it on roasted pork or duck. Or serve it warm over ice cream.

BLACKBERRY-BLACK PEPPER SPREAD

makes: 6 (½-pt.) jars
for the shelf

———

hands-on time: 45 min.

———

total time: 2 hours, 45 min.,
plus 1 week standing time

8   (6-oz.) packages blackberries, stems removed
¼   tsp. freshly ground pepper
1   (1¾-oz.) package powdered pectin
4½   cups sugar

1. Gently wash berries; drain and place in an 8-qt. stainless steel or enameled Dutch oven with ½ cup water. Crush berries with a potato masher. Bring to a boil, stirring constantly; reduce heat, and simmer 5 minutes or until berries are soft, stirring often. Remove from heat. Line a wire-mesh strainer with 2 layers of damp cheesecloth or a jelly bag. Place over a bowl. Pour berry mixture into strainer, and let drain 1 hour and 45 minutes or as needed to extract 3½ cups juice. (Do not press or squeeze mixture.) Discard solids. Return juice to Dutch oven. Stir in pepper.

2. Sterilize jars, and prepare lids as described on page 22.

3. While jars are boiling, stir pectin into juice mixture. Bring to a rolling boil, stirring constantly. Stir in sugar; return to a rolling boil, and boil 1 minute. Remove from heat; let foam settle (about 1 minute). Skim off and discard any foam.

4. Fill, seal, and process jars as described on pages 22–25, leaving ¼-inch headspace and processing 5 minutes.

5. Remove jars from water, and let stand, undisturbed, at room temperature 24 hours. To check seals, remove the bands, and press down on the center of each lid. If the lid doesn't move, the jar is sealed. If the lid depresses and pops up again, the jar is not sealed. Store properly sealed jars in a cool, dark place up to 1 year. Refrigerate after opening.

little jars, big flavors

A hint of peppery-sweet ginger sets this recipe apart from Grandmama's. Spread it on toasted baguette slices for a sunny start to the day.

PEACH-GINGER BUTTER

5 cups coarsely chopped fresh peaches (2½ lb., about 6 medium)

¼ cup finely chopped crystallized ginger

1 tsp. lemon zest
1 Tbsp. fresh lemon juice
1½ cups sugar

makes: 3 (½-pt.) jars
for the shelf

———

hands-on time: 55 min.

———

total time: 55 min.,
plus 1 week standing time

1. Combine first 4 ingredients and ¼ cup water in a 6-qt. stainless steel or enameled Dutch oven. Bring to a boil over medium-high heat, stirring often. Reduce heat, and simmer, uncovered, 15 minutes or until peaches are tender, stirring occasionally. Remove from heat, and let cool slightly. Place peach mixture in a food processor; pulse until almost smooth.

2. Sterilize jars, and prepare lids as described on page 22.

3. While jars are boiling, combine peach puree and sugar in a large stainless steel saucepan. Bring to a boil over medium heat, stirring until sugar dissolves. Cook, stirring constantly, 23 minutes or until mixture thickens and holds its shape on a spoon.

4. Fill, seal, and process jars as described on pages 22–25, leaving ¼-inch headspace and processing 10 minutes.

5. Remove jars from water, and let stand, undisturbed, at room temperature 24 hours. To check seals, remove the bands, and press down on the center of each lid. If the lid doesn't move, the jar is sealed. If the lid depresses and pops up again, the jar is not sealed. Store properly sealed jars in a cool, dark place up to 1 year. Refrigerate after opening.

little jars, big flavors

This butter is the epitome of waste-not-want-not Southern thrift. You make it with the blueberry pulp that's left over from making our delicious Blueberry Syrup (page 223).

BLUEBERRY BUTTER

5½ cups blueberry pulp reserved from Blueberry Syrup (page 223)

3 cups sugar

1½ Tbsp. fresh lemon juice

1 Tbsp. lemon zest

¼ tsp. ground nutmeg

1. Process blueberry pulp in a food processor 1 minute or until very smooth. Combine pureed pulp, sugar, and remaining ingredients in an 8-qt. stainless steel or enameled Dutch oven. Bring to a boil over medium heat, stirring often. Reduce heat, and simmer, stirring constantly, 35 to 40 minutes or until mixture thickens and holds its shape on a spoon.

2. While blueberry mixture cooks, sterilize jars, and prepare lids as described on page 22.

3. Fill, seal, and process jars as described on pages 22–25, leaving ¼-inch headspace and processing 10 minutes.

4. Remove jars from water, and let stand, undisturbed, at room temperature 24 hours. To check seals, remove the bands, and press down on the center of each lid. If the lid doesn't move, the jar is sealed. If the lid depresses and pops up again, the jar is not sealed. Store properly sealed jars in a cool, dark place up to 1 year. Refrigerate after opening.

makes: 6 (½-pt.) jars
for the shelf

hands-on time: 1 hour, 15 min.

total time: 1 hour, 25 min.,
plus 1 week standing time

Use this on muffins and scones, as a condiment on a cheese platter, or as a filling for hand pies. For the best texture and flavor, start with pears that are sweet and ripe but firm enough to squeeze without squishing.

PEAR-STAR ANISE BUTTER

3¾ lb. firm, ripe Anjou pears, peeled, cored, and coarsely chopped (6½ cups)

3¾ tsp. orange zest

⅓ cup fresh orange juice

2½ tsp. lemon zest

2 Tbsp. fresh lemon juice

1½ cups sugar

½ tsp. freshly grated nutmeg

4 star anise

makes: 4 (½-pt.) jars
for the shelf

hands-on time: 55 min.

total time: 1 hour, 15 min.,
plus 1 week standing time

1. Bring first 5 ingredients and ¼ cup water to a boil in a large stainless steel saucepan. Reduce heat, and simmer, uncovered, 20 to 25 minutes or until pears are soft, stirring occasionally.

2. Place pear mixture in a food processor, and pulse 12 times or until coarsely pureed.

3. Sterilize jars, and prepare lids as described on page 22.

4. While jars are boiling, bring 3⅓ cups pear puree, sugar, and nutmeg to a boil in saucepan, stirring until sugar dissolves. Reduce heat, and simmer 20 minutes or until mixture is thickened and holds its shape on a spoon.

5. Place 1 star anise in each hot jar, and spoon hot mixture into hot sterilized jars, leaving ¼-inch headspace. Seal and process jars as described on pages 22–25, processing 10 minutes.

6. Remove jars from water, and let stand, undisturbed, at room temperature 24 hours. To check seals, remove the bands, and press down on the center of each lid. If the lid doesn't move, the jar is sealed. If the lid depresses and pops up again, the jar is not sealed. Store properly sealed jars in a cool, dark place up to 1 year. Remove star anise, and refrigerate butter after opening.

little jars, big flavors

MARMALADES, PRESERVES & DRUNKEN FRUIT

This sunny marmalade has more perk and less bite than what's commonly sold. A tiny bit of baking soda helps soften the rind.

GRAPEFRUIT MARMALADE

3	large red grapefruit (about 2¾ lb.)	1	(1¾-oz.) package powdered pectin
1	lemon		
⅛	tsp. baking soda	4	cups sugar

1. Scrub fruit thoroughly; rinse well, and pat dry. Carefully strip rind from grapefruit and lemon with a vegetable peeler, avoiding bitter white pith. Coarsely chop rind to measure 1 cup. Place rind, 2½ cups water, and baking soda in a 6-qt. stainless steel or enameled Dutch oven. Bring to a boil over high heat; cover, reduce heat, and simmer, stirring occasionally, 20 minutes.

2. While rind simmers, sterilize jars, and prepare lids as described on page 22. While the jars are boiling, prepare the fruit. Using a sharp, thin-bladed knife, cut a ¼-inch-thick slice from each end of grapefruit and lemon. Place flat-end down on a cutting board, and remove and discard peel (bitter white pith and any remaining rind) in strips, cutting from top to bottom, and following the curvature of the fruit. Holding peeled fruit in the palm of your hand and working over bowl to collect juices, slice between membranes, and gently remove whole segments. Discard membranes and seeds. Coarsely chop fruit to measure 2¼ cups fruit and juices.

3. Add fruit and juices to rind. Bring to a boil; reduce heat, and simmer, uncovered, stirring often, 10 minutes. Stir in pectin. Bring to a boil; stir in sugar. Bring to a rolling boil; boil 1 minute, stirring constantly. Remove from heat; let foam settle (about 1 minute). Skim off and discard any foam.

4. Fill, seal, and process jars as described on pages 22–25, leaving ¼-inch headspace and processing 10 minutes.

5. Remove jars from water, and let stand, undisturbed, at room temperature 24 hours. To check seals, remove the bands, and press down on the center of each lid. If the lid doesn't move, the jar is sealed. If the lid depresses and pops up again, the jar is not sealed. Store properly sealed jars in a cool, dark place up to 1 year. Refrigerate after opening.

makes: 4 (½-pt.) jars for the shelf

hands-on time: 1 hour

total time: 1 hour, 15 min., plus 1 week standing time

little jars, big flavors

Grapefruit
Marmalade
July 2012

We think this marmalade tastes good right out of the pot, better after one week in the jar, and fantastic after three weeks.

PEACH-ORANGE MARMALADE

4   to 5 large navel oranges
8   cups chopped peeled peaches
    (about 6 lb. whole peaches)

2   Tbsp. lemon juice
5   cups sugar

makes: 7 (½-pt.) jars
for the shelf

hands-on time: 1 hour, 20 min.

total time: 1 hour, 35 min.,
plus 3 weeks standing time

1. Scrub oranges thoroughly; rinse well, and pat dry. Strip rind from oranges with a vegetable peeler, avoiding bitter white pith. Thinly slice rind to measure ¾ cup. Remove any remaining white pith from oranges. Using a sharp, thin-bladed knife, cut a ¼-inch-thick slice from each end of oranges. Place flat-end down on a cutting board, and remove and discard peel (bitter white pith and any remaining rind) in strips, cutting from top to bottom, and following the curvature of the fruit. Holding peeled fruit in the palm of your hand and working over bowl to collect juices, slice between membranes, and gently remove whole segments. Discard membranes and seeds. Chop sections to measure 1½ cups chopped fruit and juice.

2. Combine chopped orange sections and juice, rind, peaches, and next 2 ingredients in an 8-qt. stainless steel or enameled Dutch oven. Bring to a boil over medium heat, stirring occasionally until sugar dissolves. Boil 45 to 50 minutes or until thickened, stirring frequently to prevent sticking. Meanwhile, sterilize jars, and prepare lids as described on page 22. Remove thickened mixture from heat; let foam settle (about 1 minute). Skim off and discard any foam.

3. Fill hot jars with hot mixture, seal, and process as described on pages 22–25, leaving ¼-inch headspace and processing 10 minutes.

4. Remove jars from water, and let stand, undisturbed, at room temperature 24 hours. To check seals, remove the bands, and press down on the center of each lid. If the lid doesn't move, the jar is sealed. If the lid depresses and pops up again, the jar is not sealed. Store properly sealed jars in a cool, dark place up to 1 year. Refrigerate after opening.

Sparkling rosé lends color and a flavor twist to this marmalade, which is as at home on the brunch table as the drink for which it's named. Though it requires a longish simmer to thicken, it's designed for the fridge rather than the shelf and needs only a day of chilling before it reaches its full flavor. Pour yourself a cup of coffee, and dream up the rest of your brunch menu while tomorrow's marmalade bubbles away.

MIMOSA MARMALADE

4	large navel oranges	⅛	tsp. kosher salt
1	large lemon	1¾	cups sparkling rosé or
2	cups sugar		sparkling white wine

1. Scrub fruit thoroughly; rinse well, and pat dry. Grate zest from oranges to equal 2 Tbsp. Grate zest from lemon to equal 1 tsp.

2. Using a sharp, thin-bladed knife, cut a ¼-inch-thick slice from each end of oranges and lemon. Place flat-end down on a cutting board, and remove and discard peel (bitter white pith and any remaining zest) in strips, cutting from top to bottom, and following the curvature of the fruit. Holding peeled fruit in the palm of your hand and working over bowl to collect juices, slice between membranes, and gently remove whole segments. Reserve segments and ⅓ cup juice. Discard membranes and seeds.

3. Stir together zest, reserved whole segments and juice, sugar, and next 2 ingredients in a heavy-bottomed 4-qt. stainless steel saucepan or enameled Dutch oven. Bring to a boil over medium-high heat, stirring occasionally until sugar dissolves. Reduce heat, and simmer, stirring occasionally, 1 hour or until mixture is slightly thickened and a candy thermometer registers 225°. Remove from heat. Let foam settle (about 1 minute). Skim off and discard any foam.

4. Spoon mixture into clean canning jars or other heatproof containers with lids. Cool completely (about 1 hour; mixture will thicken more as it cools). Cover and chill 24 hours before serving. Store in refrigerator up to 3 weeks.

makes: 2 (½-pt.) jars
for the fridge

hands-on time: 1 hour, 30 min.

total time: 2 hours, 30 min.,
plus 1 day for chilling

CITRUS-VANILLA BEAN MARMALADE

4	large navel oranges	4	cups sugar
4	large red grapefruit (about 3¾ lb.)	¼	tsp. kosher salt
2	large lemons	2	vanilla beans, split lengthwise

1. Scrub fruit thoroughly; rinse well, and pat dry. Grate zest from oranges to equal 2 Tbsp. Grate zest from grapefruit to equal 2 Tbsp. Grate zest from lemon to equal 2 tsp. Using a sharp, thin-bladed knife, cut a ¼-inch-thick slice from each end of oranges, grapefruit, and lemons. Working with 1 piece of fruit at a time, place flat-end down on a cutting board, and remove peel (bitter white pith and any remaining zest) in strips, cutting from top to bottom, and following the curvature of fruit. Holding peeled fruit in the palm of your hand and working over bowl to collect juices, slice between membranes, and gently remove whole segments. Reserve 4½ cups whole segments and ½ cup juice. Discard membranes and seeds.

2. Stir together 3½ cups water, citrus zest, reserved citrus segments and juice, sugar, and salt in a 6-qt. stainless steel or enameled Dutch oven. Scrape seeds from vanilla bean; add seeds and bean to citrus mixture. Bring to a boil over medium-high heat, stirring until sugar dissolves. Reduce heat, and simmer, stirring occasionally, 55 minutes or until mixture is slightly thickened and a candy thermometer registers 225°.

3. While mixture simmers, sterilize jars, and prepare lids as described on page 22. Remove mixture from heat. Remove and discard vanilla beans. Let foam settle (about 1 minute). Skim off and discard any foam. Fill hot jars with hot mixture, seal, and process as described on pages 22–25, leaving ¼-inch headspace and processing 10 minutes.

4. Remove jars from water, and let jars stand, undisturbed, at room temperature 24 hours. To check seals, remove the bands and press down on the center of each lid. If the lid doesn't move, the jar is sealed. If the lid depresses and pops up again, the jar is not sealed. Store properly sealed jars in a cool, dark place up to 1 year. Refrigerate after opening.

makes: 5 (½-pt.) jars
for the shelf

hands-on time: 2 hours, 17 min.

total time: 2 hours, 17 min.,
plus 1 week standing time

NOTE: Use a Dutch oven with high sides to minimize splattering while the fruit mixture simmers.

little jars, big flavors

Fat nuggets of fig, toothsome slices of lemon, and a few sprigs of fresh thyme make these preserves positively enchanting.

CHUNKY LEMON-FIG PRESERVES

3   lb. brown turkey figs, stems removed
1   small lemon
4   cups sugar
¼   cup lemon juice
Parchment paper or wax paper
3   thyme sprigs
Kitchen string

makes: 7 (½-pt.) jars for the shelf

——

hands-on time: 1 hour, 5 min.

——

total time: 14 hours, 35 min., plus 1 week standing time

1. Rinse figs under cold running water; drain and pat dry. Cut figs into quarters if large, halves if small. Quarter lemon lengthwise, and remove seeds; thinly slice the quarters crosswise. Layer fig pieces, sugar, and lemon slices alternately in a 6-qt. stainless steel or enameled Dutch oven. Add lemon juice and 2 cups water. Bring to a boil without stirring.

2. Remove from heat, and let cool to room temperature (about 1 hour, 30 minutes). Place a piece of parchment or wax paper directly on mixture, and chill 12 hours.

3. Bring chilled mixture in Dutch oven to a boil. Boil, stirring occasionally and skimming and discarding foam from surface, 30 minutes or until figs and lemon slices are translucent and syrup has thickened slightly. While mixture boils, sterilize jars, and prepare lids as described on page 22.

4. Tie thyme sprigs together with kitchen string; add to fig mixture. Continue boiling, stirring occasionally, 10 minutes or until mixture passes the drip or saucer tests on page 26. Remove from heat. Discard thyme stems and string. Let foam settle (about 1 minute). Skim off and discard any foam.

5. Fill hot jars with hot mixture; seal, and process jars as described on pages 22–25, leaving ¼-inch headspace and processing 5 minutes.

6. Remove jars from water, and let stand, undisturbed, at room temperature 24 hours. To check seals, remove the bands, and press down on the center of each lid. If the lid doesn't move, the jar is sealed. If the lid depresses and pops up again, the jar is not sealed. Store properly sealed jars in a cool, dark place up to 1 year. Refrigerate after opening.

There is, indeed, an herb called pineapple sage. It smells and tastes just as it sounds: like the happy marriage of the sweet tropical fruit and the hearty Thanksgiving herb. These preserves achieve a similar effect with plain old pineapple and garden-variety sage. Try some as a sauce with baked ham or grilled trout, a topping for a banana split, or a filling for our delicious Vanilla Bean–Pineapple-Sage Layer Cake (page 86).

PINEAPPLE-SAGE PRESERVES

1   (1-lb.) fresh pineapple, peeled and cored

¼   cup loosely packed fresh sage leaves, rinsed, dried, and tied in cheesecloth

3   Tbsp. lemon juice

3¼ cups sugar

1   (3-oz.) package liquid pectin

makes: about 4 (½-pt.) jars for the shelf

hands-on time: 40 min.

total time: 1 hour, 5 min., plus 1 week standing time

1. Sterilize jars, and prepare lids as described on page 22.

2. While jars are boiling, chop pineapple to measure 2½ cups pineapple and juice. Place in a 6-qt. stainless steel or enameled Dutch oven. Add sage, and bring to a boil; remove from heat, cover, and steep 10 minutes. Remove and discard sage and cheesecloth. Stir in lemon juice and sugar. Bring to a rolling boil over high heat, stirring constantly. Boil for 1 minute, stirring constantly. Remove from heat; stir in pectin. Let foam settle (about 1 minute). Skim off and discard any foam.

3. Fill, seal, and process jars as described on pages 22–25, leaving ¼-inch headspace and processing 10 minutes.

4. Remove jars from water, and let stand, undisturbed, at room temperature 24 hours. To check seals, remove the bands, and press down on the center of each lid. If the lid doesn't move, the jar is sealed. If the lid depresses and pops up again, the jar is not sealed. Store properly sealed jars in a cool, dark place up to 1 year. Refrigerate after opening.

little jars, big flavors

VANILLA BEAN-PINEAPPLE-SAGE LAYER CAKE

makes: 16 servings
for the table

hands-on time: 32 min.

total time: 2 hours, 5 min.

NOTE: Try this cake with your favorite jam or preserves. You can substitute vanilla extract for the vanilla bean paste.

CAKE:
Parchment paper
1   cup butter, softened
½   cup shortening
2   cups sugar
4   large eggs
2¾ cups all-purpose soft-wheat flour
2   tsp. baking powder
¼   tsp. salt
1   cup buttermilk
1   Tbsp. vanilla bean paste

FROSTING:
1   cup heavy whipping cream
12 oz. mascarpone cheese, softened
1   cup powdered sugar
1   tsp. vanilla bean paste
⅛   tsp. salt
1½ cups Pineapple-Sage Preserves (page 85)
Garnish: fresh fruit

1. Preheat oven to 350°. Lightly grease 3 (9-inch) round cake pans; line bottoms with parchment paper, and lightly grease paper.

2. Prepare Cake: Beat butter and shortening at medium speed with an electric mixer until creamy. Gradually add sugar, beating well. Add eggs, 1 at a time, beating until blended after each addition. Combine flour, baking powder, and salt; add to butter mixture alternately with buttermilk, beginning and ending with flour mixture. Beat at low speed until blended after each addition. Stir in vanilla bean paste. Pour batter into prepared pans.

3. Bake at 350° for 20 to 23 minutes or until a wooden pick inserted in center comes out clean. Remove from oven, and gently run a knife around outer edge of cake layers to loosen from sides of pans. Cool in pans on wire racks 10 minutes. Remove from pans to wire racks; discard parchment paper. Cool completely (about 1 hour).

4. Prepare Frosting: Beat cream at high speed with an electric mixer until soft peaks form. In a separate bowl, beat cheese and next 3 ingredients at medium speed until blended. Add cheese mixture to whipped cream; beat on low speed just until blended and stiff peaks form. (Do not overbeat.)

5. Place 1 cake layer on a serving plate; spread top with half of preserves. Top with second cake layer; spread top with remaining preserves. Top with last cake layer. Spread top and sides of cake with frosting. Garnish, if desired.

No need to heat up your kitchen for this recipe; the cooking happens entirely in the microwave, and you store it in the fridge.

MICROWAVE NECTARINE-GINGER PRESERVES

5   cups diced unpeeled nectarines (2¾ lb.)
1½ cups sugar
⅓ cup minced crystallized ginger
3   Tbsp. lemon juice
1   (1¾-oz.) package powdered pectin

1. Stir together all ingredients in a 4-qt. microwave-safe glass bowl. Microwave, uncovered, at HIGH 8 minutes (mixture will boil); stir.

2. Microwave at HIGH 10 to 12 minutes or until liquid is the viscosity of pancake syrup. (Mixture will thicken to soft-set preserves after it cools and chills.) Cool completely (about 2 hours).

3. Serve immediately, or spoon into clean canning jars or other airtight containers with lids. Cover and chill. Store in refrigerator up to 3 weeks.

makes: 3 (½-pt.) jars for the fridge

hands-on time: 30 min.

total time: 2 hours, 30 min.

little jars, big flavors

A bit of balsamic vinegar gives plums a boost in these microwave-to-fridge preserves. You can easily omit the basil, if desired, since it's stirred in at the end of the cooking.

MICROWAVE BALSAMIC-PLUM PRESERVES

makes: 3 (½-pt.) jars
for the fridge

hands-on time: 30 min.

total time: 2 hr., 30 min.

5	cups diced unpeeled red plums (2½ lb.)
1½	cups sugar
3	Tbsp. balsamic vinegar
1	(1¾-oz.) package powdered pectin
1	Tbsp. chopped fresh basil

1. Stir together first 4 ingredients in a 4-qt. microwave-safe glass bowl. Microwave, uncovered, at HIGH 8 minutes (mixture will boil); stir.

2. Microwave at HIGH 10 to 12 minutes or until liquid is the viscosity of pancake syrup. (Mixture will thicken to soft-set preserves after it cools and chills.) Stir in basil. Cool completely (about 2 hours).

3. Serve immediately, or spoon into clean canning jars or other airtight containers with lids. Cover and chill. Store in refrigerator up to 3 weeks.

Try these on grilled baguette slices (pictured at right) or in our tartlets (recipe on next page).

MICROWAVE TOMATO-PEACH PRESERVES

2½ cups diced peeled peaches (1¼ lb.)
2½ cups seeded and diced plum tomatoes (5 medium)
1½ cups sugar
3 Tbsp. lemon juice
1 (1¾-oz.) package powdered pectin
1½ tsp. minced fresh rosemary
½ tsp. freshly ground pepper

1. Stir together first 5 ingredients in a 4-qt. microwave-safe glass bowl. Microwave, uncovered, at HIGH 8 minutes (mixture will boil); stir.

2. Microwave at HIGH 12 to 16 minutes or until liquid is the viscosity of pancake syrup. (Mixture will thicken to soft-set preserves after it cools.) Stir rosemary and pepper into warm preserves. Cool completely (about 2 hours).

3. Serve immediately, or spoon into clean canning jars or other airtight containers with lids. Cover and chill. Store in refrigerator up to 3 weeks.

NOTE: For thicker preserves, microwave at HIGH 16 minutes or until slightly thickened in step 2.

makes: 3 (½-pt.) jars
for the fridge

hands-on time: 35 min.

total time: 2 hours, 35 min.

GOAT CHEESE TARTLETS WITH TOMATO-PEACH PRESERVES

2   (1.9-oz.) packages frozen mini-phyllo
    pastry shells (30 shells), thawed
4   oz. cream cheese, softened
1   (4-oz.) package goat cheese, softened
1   large egg
1   Tbsp. whipping cream
¼   tsp. salt
⅛   tsp. freshly ground pepper
1   cup Microwave Tomato-Peach Preserves
    (on previous page)

1. Preheat oven to 350°. Arrange phyllo shells in a single layer on a jelly-roll pan.

2. Beat cream cheese and goat cheese at medium speed with an electric mixer until smooth. Add egg, beating at low speed until blended. Add cream, salt, and pepper, beating at low speed until blended. Fill each shell with about 2 tsp. cheese mixture.

3. Bake at 350° for 10 to 12 minutes or until shells are lightly browned and filling is set. Top each tartlet with about 1½ tsp. preserves.

makes: 15 servings
for the table

hands-on time: 10 min.

total time: 20 min.

little jars, big flavors

Think of a conserve as a fruit preserve's nutty cousin. It's a sweet condiment containing fruit (fresh and sometimes dried too), sugar, and nuts. This one gets its rosy hue from dried cranberries and apple peels and its nuttiness from Southern pecans. Try it with roast turkey or pork, smoked chicken, or on a grilled panini with your favorite melting cheese.

HONEYCRISP APPLE-CRANBERRY CONSERVE

2¼ cups finely chopped unpeeled Honeycrisp apples

½ cup dried cranberries

2 Tbsp. lemon juice

1 (1¾-oz.) package powdered pectin

2¾ cups sugar

¼ cup chopped pecans

1. Sterilize jars, and prepare lids as described on page 22.

2. While jars are boiling, combine first 3 ingredients and ¼ cup water in a stainless steel saucepan over medium-high heat. Add pectin, and stir well. Bring to a boil, stirring constantly. Add sugar, and return to a full boil, stirring constantly. Boil 1 minute without stirring. Remove from heat. Let foam settle (about 1 minute). Skim off and discard any foam. Stir in pecans.

3. Fill, seal, and process jars as described on pages 22–25, leaving ¼-inch headspace and processing 5 minutes.

4. Remove jars from water, and let stand, undisturbed, at room temperature 24 hours. To check seals, remove the bands, and press down on the center of each lid. If the lid doesn't move, the jar is sealed. If the lid depresses and pops up again, the jar is not sealed. Store properly sealed jars in a cool, dark place up to 1 year. Refrigerate after opening.

makes: 3 (½-pt.) jars
for the shelf

hands-on time: 35 min.

total time: 45 min.,
plus 1 week standing time

little jars, big flavors

A little dab of this sweet onion marmalade is all you need to jump-start an amazing appetizer or main dish. Try it with roasted quail, pan-seared duck, grilled pork chops, or wherever caramelized onions are welcome.

DOUBLE-ONION MARMALADE

1½ cups thinly sliced red onion	Cheesecloth
1½ cups thinly sliced Vidalia onion	Kitchen string
¼ cup firmly packed light brown sugar	2½ cups unsweetened apple juice
⅓ cup cider vinegar (5% acidity)	½ cup raisins
1 Tbsp. black peppercorns	1 (1¾-oz.) package powdered pectin
2 bay leaves	4 cups sugar

1. Combine first 4 ingredients in a 6-qt. stainless steel or enameled Dutch oven. Cook, stirring often, over medium heat 13 minutes or until liquid evaporates.

2. Sterilize jars, and prepare lids as described on page 22.

3. While jars are boiling, place peppercorns and bay leaves on a 5-inch square of cheesecloth; tie with kitchen string, and add to onion mixture. Add apple juice and raisins; stir in pectin. Bring to a boil. Hold spice bag to one side of Dutch oven with tongs. Stir in sugar. Release spice bag. Bring mixture to a rolling boil; boil 1 minute, stirring constantly. Remove from heat; remove and discard spice bag. Let foam settle (about 1 minute). Skim off and discard any foam.

4. Fill, seal, and process jars as described on pages 22–25, leaving ¼-inch headspace and processing 15 minutes.

5. Remove jars from water, and let stand, undisturbed, at room temperature 24 hours. To check seals, remove the bands, and press down on the center of each lid. If the lid doesn't move, the jar is sealed. If the lid depresses and pops up again, the jar is not sealed. Store properly sealed jars in a cool, dark place up to 1 year. Refrigerate after opening.

Having a jar of these aromatic beauties on the shelf means you can have poached pears even when fresh pears aren't in season. For the prettiest results and easiest packing, choose small firm pears, use a melon baller to scoop out the cores, and pack pears tightly in widemouthed jars.

SPICED PEARS IN RED WINE

2	Tbsp. lemon juice	4	whole cloves
3½	lb. small firm, ripe Bosc pears	4	(3-inch) cinnamon sticks
3	cups dry red wine	4	star anise
3	cups sugar		

makes: 4 widemouthed (1-pt.) jars for the shelf

hands-on time: 1 hour

total time: 1 hour, 15 min., plus 1 week standing time

1. Combine 8 cups water and lemon juice in a large bowl. Peel, halve, and core pears; place them immediately in lemon juice mixture to prevent browning.

2. Sterilize jars, and prepare lids as described on page 22.

3. While jars are boiling, cook wine and sugar in a medium stainless steel saucepan over medium heat, stirring until sugar dissolves. Reduce heat and allow to simmer while packing jars.

4. Place 1 clove, 1 cinnamon stick, and 1 star anise in each hot jar. Remove 2 to 3 pear halves from lemon juice mixture, and pack bottom-ends down into 1 jar; remove 2 or 3 more pear halves from lemon juice mixture, and tightly pack bottom-ends up into jar. Repeat with remaining pears and jars.

5. Bring wine mixture to a boil; pour over pears, leaving ½-inch headspace. Seal and process jars as described on pages 22–25, processing 20 minutes.

6. Remove jars from water, and let stand, undisturbed, at room temperature 24 hours. To check seals, remove the bands, and press down on the center of each lid. If the lid doesn't move, the jar is sealed. If the lid depresses and pops up again, the jar is not sealed. Store properly sealed jars in a cool, dark place up to 1 year. Refrigerate after opening.

little jars, big flavors

This wine-spiked fruit holds its own as a dessert, but you also can spoon the fruit and syrup over pound cake, cheesecake, and ice cream.

SANGRÍA FRUIT

1 (750-milliliter) bottle Moscato or other sweet white wine
¼ cup orange liqueur
1 small orange, unpeeled
1 small peach or nectarine, peeled and cut into 6 wedges
1 plum, cut into 6 wedges
16 fresh figs, stemmed and halved
½ cup seedless red grapes
½ cup seedless green grapes

makes: 3 (1-pt.) jars for the fridge

hands-on time: 15 min.

total time: 2 hours, 35 min., plus 2 days for chilling

1. Bring wine to a boil in a 3-qt. stainless steel saucepan. Boil 20 to 23 minutes or until reduced to 1½ cups. Remove from heat; stir in orange liqueur.

2. Cut orange in half horizontally; slice crosswise into ¼-inch-thick slices. Mix gently with remaining fruit.

3. Pack fruit tightly into clean (1-pt.) jars or other heatproof, nonmetallic containers with lids, leaving ¼-inch headspace. Cover fruit with hot wine mixture. Apply lids, and let cool 2 hours.

4. Chill at least 2 days before serving. Store in refrigerator up to 2 weeks.

Bourbon and other fine spirits do double duty when it comes to fruit, acting as both preservative and flavor booster. Try these boozy babies straight up for dessert, blended into a cocktail, or layered in our adult Drunken Peach Ice Cream Sundaes (page 104).

DRUNKEN PEACHES

1	lemon	6	(¼-inch) orange slices
4½	lb. fresh freestone peaches		(from 2 small navel oranges)
2½	cups sugar	¾	cup bourbon
3	vanilla beans, halved crosswise		

1. Bring a large pot of water to a boil. Fill a large bowl two-thirds full of ice water. Cut lemon in half, and squeeze juice into ice water. Working in batches, place peaches in a wire basket, lower into boiling water, and blanch 60 seconds. Place immediately in lemon juice mixture. When cool enough to handle, peel peaches, cut in half, and remove pits. Cut each half into 4 wedges; return to lemon juice mixture.

2. Sterilize jars, and prepare lids as described on page 22. While jars are boiling, stir together sugar and 3 cups water in a large saucepan. Split vanilla bean halves lengthwise; scrape out seeds. Add vanilla bean and seeds to sugar mixture; cook over medium-high heat, stirring until sugar dissolves. Bring to and maintain at a low simmer.

3. Place 1 orange slice and 1 vanilla bean half into each hot jar. Drain peach quarters, and pack tightly into hot jars. Ladle hot syrup into jars, leaving 1½-inch headspace. Add 2 Tbsp. bourbon to each jar. Add more syrup to the jars, leaving ½-inch headspace. Seal and process jars as described on pages 22–25, processing 25 minutes.

4. Remove jars from water, and let stand, undisturbed, at room temperature 24 hours. To check seals, remove the bands, and press down on the center of each lid. If the lid doesn't move, the jar is sealed. If the lid depresses and pops up again, the jar is not sealed. Store properly sealed jars in a cool, dark place up to 1 year. Refrigerate after opening.

makes: 6 (1-pt.) jars
for the shelf

hands-on time: 1 hour

total time: 1 hour, 30 min.,
plus 3 weeks standing time

NOTE: Peaches that don't cling to their pits work best, and slices from smaller oranges look prettier in the jars.

little jars, big flavors

The Cinnamon-Praline Cracker Candy part of this recipe makes more than you're likely to need for four sundaes. Store any remaining candy in an airtight container for up to a week.

DRUNKEN PEACH
ICE CREAM SUNDAES

CINNAMON-PRALINE CRACKER CANDY:

1½ cup coarsely chopped pecans

13 cinnamon graham cracker sheets

Parchment paper

¾ cup firmly packed light brown sugar

¾ cup butter

SUNDAES:

1 qt. vanilla ice cream

1 pt. Drunken Peaches (page 103)

1. Prepare Cinnamon-Praline Cracker Candy: Preheat oven to 350°. Bake pecans in a single layer in a shallow pan 10 to 12 minutes or until toasted and fragrant, stirring halfway through.

2. Arrange graham crackers snugly in a single layer on a parchment paper-lined 15- x 10-inch jelly-roll pan. Heat brown sugar and butter in a saucepan over medium heat until melted and smooth, stirring constantly (about 3 minutes). Pour sugar mixture over crackers; spread evenly.

3. Bake at 350° for 10 minutes; reduce oven temperature to 325°, and bake 12 more minutes. Remove from oven; sprinkle with pecans, pressing lightly. Cool completely on a wire rack (about 30 minutes). Break candy into small pieces.

4. Prepare Sundaes: Layer 1 cup ice cream, ½ cup Drunken Peaches, and desired amount of Cinnamon-Praline Cracker Candy in each of 4 bowls. Serve immediately.

PUTTING-UP PARTIES

4

PUTTING ON A PUTTING-UP PARTY

• ◆ •

BY VIRGINIA WILLIS

Imagine the ultimate DIY event: a joyful gathering of friends making delicious and beautiful food from scratch. The scent of fresh dill and hard spices hangs in the air, and brightly colored fruits and vegetables fill the tables. The soundtrack for this shindig? Glass jars clinking in a sink full of sudsy water. The tinny staccato of metal bowls being stacked. Giggles and laughter punctuated by the timer bell. Everyone leaves with a collection of preserves to stash or share. Just thinking about a putting-up party makes me smile. Many hands make light work, but the main reason I love a putting-up party? It makes canning downright fun.

Once upon a time, it was all hands on deck to "put up" food during harvest. I remember my grandparents, aunts, and mother working together in a steamy kitchen late into the night, prepping vegetables for the jar or the freezer. In my youth, no one escaped a canning session when the garden came in. Everyone was roped into shelling peas, shucking corn, and snapping beans.

It was hard work, but what satisfaction! When we were done, Mason jars of peach jam, blackberry preserves, green beans, pickles, pears, and chowchow stood in neat lines, like soldiers, on the wooden basement shelves.

Those memories are precious to me now. I'm fairly certain that my love of food and cooking took root in our simple country kitchen. Mama taught me to blanch green vegetables before placing them in containers so they would freeze better and not to squeeze the jelly bag so as to not make the jelly cloudy. I relish the passing-down of kitchen traditions and recipes like my grandmother's bread-and-butter pickles and my mother's Scuppernong jelly.

It might sound like I was born with a candy thermometer in one hand and a Mason jar in the other, but canning wasn't always easy for me. Yes, I grew up with canning and preserving. Yes, I am now a professional chef. But as a teenager, I didn't fully enjoy canning. And in Mama's kitchen I was a mere prep

little jars, big flavors

cook, several steps removed from the chef and truly terrified of the pressure canner. My preserving breakthrough occurred not during my formative years in Georgia but one summer in France, when I attended École de Cuisine La Varenne. The culinary school's director, Anne Willan, assumed that a Southerner like me would already know all about canning and preserving. I had barely tied on an apron when she pointed me in the direction of the garden and sent me to the cellar for a case of jars. (Gulp!) My first batches were nerve-wracking. Would the jelly set? Would the pickles be too soft? But one success led to another, and one evening near the end of summer I had a revelation. I was preparing dinner for a party of 20 and comfortably putting up cherry jelly at the same time when it hit me: Canning and preserving truly are not that hard.

I look at preserving now as an important cooking skill, one I pull out not just in August but whenever it makes sense, even if it's just a couple of jars. If I'm going out of town and have too much in the fridge, I'll see what I can freeze, pickle, bottle, or jar instead of tossing out. If a friend with a prolific fig tree offers me some, I preserve whatever I can't eat before they'll spoil. Putting up also just feels like a natural part of good eating. "Foodie" or not, who doesn't crave local foods and the vibrant flavors captured when you preserve them in their prime?

Finding time for the kind of mass canning my family did is difficult. But a putting-up party with a few food-loving friends feels like a manageable, small-batch version of that worthwhile tradition. As a grown-up, I think of these canning sessions less as chores and more like dinner parties with dividends.

THE BIG IDEA

Simply put, putting-up parties are social events with a practical side: You invite some friends to your home and ask each to bring the ingredients for one canning or preserving recipe. You spend a few hours catching up, putting up, and messing up just one kitchen. Everyone leaves with a variety of goodies to enjoy at home or share with family and friends.

It's faster and more fun to can several recipes with friends than to make them all on your own. Because there's some multitasking involved in canning—timing the steps just right so you get hot food in hot jars—it often goes smoother and faster with another set of hands. And isn't it nice to have someone to chat with while you ponder life and peel the peaches?

Putting-up parties introduce new recipes and unique flavors to your repertoire. You get to make and sample several recipes and find the ones you like best, while sharing the cost and effort with your friends. And, instead of canning all day to get 20 jars of the same thing (and perhaps more than you're likely to use up in a year), you leave with several different items to enjoy.

Summer is the prime time of year for preserving, but you can host a putting-up party or find something to can in any season. Spring yields pickled asparagus and strawberry jam. Summer overflows with fruits and vegetables to pickle. Fall brings apples and pears for jellies and fruit butters. Even cold winter months offer opportunities: making marmalades from onions or transforming lemons into limoncello. In fact, when it's cooler outside it's often more enjoyable to be in a warm kitchen with others.

little jars, big flavors

THE PLAN

Speaking of cool, there's something to be said for starting the party early in the day. While it always depends on everyone's schedule, I think a weekend event makes the most sense. Jams and pickles require some prep. Green beans need to be washed and trimmed; plums need to be pitted; strawberries need to be hulled. You want to make sure that you have plenty of time to complete the steps and enjoy yourselves.

The number of people to invite? That will depend on your comfort level and the size and outfitting of your kitchen. Canning doesn't require a fancy, gourmet kitchen, but there are practical considerations like the size of the sink and the number of burners on the stove-top. You will need plenty of kitchen counter and table space for people to work. You can extend the kitchen to other workspaces, such as a table on the porch or a card table in the backyard. If you're completely new to canning and preserving, I suggest you start small: two to four friends and two to four recipes.

The key to a putting-up party, or any party really, is to make a plan and tackle it a little at a time. Because I'm comfortable with canning, I tend to be less scripted about such things. (I'm likely to make a plan at the farmers' market and just call a few friends on the way home.) However, until you get the hang of it, you might want to start plotting your putting-up party up to a month ahead. Here's a step-by-step schedule to get you there.

Four Weeks Out
☐ Invite some friends. Mail, email, social media, and phone invites are all acceptable, but RSVPs are a must. Ask guests to note any food allergies or dietary restrictions with their RSVP.

Three Weeks Out
☐ Plan a snacks menu and discuss with your RSVP'd guests what to preserve; gather your snacks recipes with an eye toward those that can be prepared in advance, or even frozen, with just simple warming and quick assembly on the day of your putting-up party. Note how far in advance each recipe can be prepared.

☐ Make a shopping list for the snacks menu.

☐ Line up any additional help you may need; consider hiring a high school student for baby-sitting or to help with cleanup.

Two Weeks Out
☐ See what's in season and finalize your list of items to put up.

☐ Make sure you have the necessary gear for preserving (see the handy list on pages 114–115 or the pictures on pages 18–19) and serving dishes for refreshments. Coordinate with guests who are bringing ingredients, any additional equipment, and jars. Procure aprons for the guests—or ask each to bring one.

☐ Create a music playlist. Mellow background tunes help keep the atmosphere light. Have a little fun with it!

☐ Assemble or purchase a first-aid kit—just in case. Consider burn cream or an aloe plant, bandages, alcohol, and antibiotic cream.

One Week Out

☐ Clean the kitchen thoroughly, so it will need only a quick once-over before your putting-up party.

☐ Review the preserving recipes to make sure you're clear on anything that might need to be done ahead such as draining juice to make jelly.

☐ Arrange the furniture as needed for the party. Clear the dining room table and cover it with a tablecloth to use as a prep station. (Hardware stores have durable canvas drop cloths that are inexpensive and offer excellent table protection. Oilcloths and plastic tablecloths also work nicely when you're working with vegetables and fruits that stain such as beets, berries, and plums.)

Three Days Out

☐ Do a first round of grocery shopping and cooking, and prepare any snacks that can be made ahead.

☐ Remove any unnecessary kitchen appliances to clear as much space as possible.

☐ Set up a cleanup station—a box of coarse kosher salt, club soda, and a couple of kitchen towels in case a spill occurs.

☐ Designate a place for purses and overcoats.

☐ Finish grocery shopping and make a schedule for cooking any remaining snacks.

One Day Out

☐ Pull out the plates and utensils, and set up a drink station. If it's a morning party, think about coffee and stir-ins like milk, sugar, and sweetener.

☐ Chill anything you will serve cold, such as lemonade or white wine.

☐ Finish as much of the cooking and prepping for the snacks you'll serve. That will leave you and your guests free to focus on preserving and catching up.

☐ Move any frozen dishes from the freezer to the refrigerator to thaw overnight.

☐ Give your house and kitchen a final cleaning. Empty the trash and the compost bin, and make sure they're easy to find.

Day of the Putting-Up Party

☐ Finish any last-minute cooking for the snacks.

☐ Set up stations with cutting boards, peelers, colanders, and other equipment.

☐ Fill canning pots with water and set them on the stove.

☐ About 30 minutes before guests arrive, set out snacks (wrapped in plastic to ensure freshness) and beverages.

☐ Turn on the music.

☐ After guests arrive, divide the tasks to make things efficient. Put one person in charge of each recipe, perhaps. Or ask one to peel and slice, another to wash and sterilize jars, and another to set up a station near the stove for filling jars. Let others pitch in as needed.

THE GEAR

I think "share the work, share the fun" is the best approach. Consider treating this party like a cookie swap or potluck. Ask everyone to bring the produce or the main ingredient (and jars if they have them) for one recipe. As the host, you will supply snacks; basic supplies such as vinegar, sugar, canning-and-pickling salt, and labels; kitchen essentials such as cutting boards, knives, peelers, and stainless steel bowls; and basic canning equipment, including:

A canning pot and rack: This is an extra-large pot, often enameled, with a rack that holds the jars for boiling-water canning. Ball makes an affordable kit.

Canning jars, lids, and bands: These are available at hardware, grocery, and kitchen-supply stores. Two popular producers of the standard glass Mason jar are Ball and Kerr, and these brands are typically the most affordable. More expensive European jars include clamp-and-gasket types from Weck, Leifheit, and Bormioli Rocco, and glass terrines from Le Parfait. Glass jars are available in half-cup, half-pint, pint, and quart sizes. They are either regular or widemouthed, a reference to the size of the jar opening. Make certain to select the right bands and lids for your jars. Mason jars may be reused, as long as they are free of cracks and chips. (Don't use emptied mayonnaise or store-bought jelly and condiment jars, as they aren't designed for reuse.) Screwtop bands can be reused as long as they are not rusted. Lids should be used only once.

Canning tongs: Lowering the jars in and out of the hot water while keeping them upright can be tricky, but canning tongs are coated with rubber and curved to hug the jars, making lifting them in and out of hot water a breeze.

Ladles and glass measuring cups: These work best for transferring hot liquids from saucepan to jar. Heat-resistant glass measuring cups do double duty, helping you measure and pour the right amount.

Widemouthed funnel: The extra-wide mouth helps keep jar rims clean.

A few other items are nice but not essential:

Magnetic lid wand: This long plastic tool, sometimes part of a canning kit, has a magnet on the end that makes applying canning lids to the jars easy. If you don't have one, just use standard kitchen tongs.

Cooling racks: Placing hot jars directly on cold counters can crack the jars and damage countertops. Cooling racks act as a heat buffer. You can use folded towels, baking sheets, or wooden cutting boards too.

Electric teakettle: These boil water quickly without occupying a burner—awfully nice when you're out of stove and need more water in the canning pot.

little jars, big flavors

115

WHAT TO PUT UP

My family canned and preserved produce because they had an abundance of cucumbers, tomatoes, or peaches. For some gardeners (and their neighbors), that's still true. But for many today, it's a different story. When you're paying $6 a pound for heirloom tomatoes at an urban farmers' market, you want to think carefully about what to put up.

Start by talking to your invitees and seeing what's in season. For the best flavor (and often the best price), you'll want to use the freshest and most bountiful produce available.

If you're not sure what grows when in your area, check seasonal produce calendars to help you plan ahead, or ask the farmers at your local markets what's going to be good a few weeks out.

Look through this cookbook for inspiration, and consider the time and effort involved in each recipe. Jam and pickle recipes tend to be short and sweet. Jellies and marmalades may require more time for fruit to be juiced or for citrus rinds to steep.

Aim for a variety of flavors so that everyone will have a well-rounded box of goodies to take home: a fruit jam or jelly, a pickle, an infused liquor, a vegetable relish. Consider using a variety of preserving techniques—refrigerator, freezer, and boiling-water canning—to help stretch the amount you can do in a small kitchen in one day.

Dedicate some recipes to the canning pot, but don't forget about the microwave, the food processor, or even the liquor cabinet. Refrigerator and freezer preserves tend to come together more quickly than boiling-water processed recipes.

Keep it simple, settling on two to four recipes per party. Though it's tempting to add to your list when you see beautiful figs at the farmers' market, if they're not in your plan, save them for another day.

Depending on the complexity of the recipes you and your guests choose, you might even do just one or two recipes and make multiple batches of each. There's no shame in keeping it small and in saying: "This Saturday, we'll be making Mixed Berry Jam and Pickled Okra. Y'all come!"

Worth noting: Not all recipes double or triple well. A single batch of marmalade may take roughly an hour to cook down; a triple batch of marmalade may take roughly forever to cook down. It's best to actually make separate batches rather than just multiplying the ingredient amounts and proceeding in the same pot.

SNACKS FOR THE PUTTER-UPPERS

Since your kitchen will be full and busy, you want to make sure to prepare foods for your fellow canners before they arrive.

Make snacks and nibbles ahead to keep it simple. Consider recipes that require few utensils or that can be eaten out of hand. You'll have enough dishes to do when your kitchen is in canning mode!

Opt for small plates and snacks, not a big meal. Think grazing. Set up a simple buffet and take a dedicated break to eat while the jars cool or the jelly bag hangs.

Turn the page for seasonal menu ideas for what to preserve and what to serve.

SPRING

Putting-Up Party

WHAT TO PUT UP	WHAT TO SERVE
Mint Jelly (page 63)	Ginger ale
Strawberry-Rhubarb Freezer Jam (page 206)	Green salad
Strawberry-Basil Jam (page 41)	Caramelized Onion and Bacon Quiche (next page)
Strawberry-Port Jam (page 42)	Strawberry Shortcakes (page 121)
Pickled Asparagus (page 168)	
Pickled Japanese Turnips with Shiso (page 158)	
Pickled Rainbow Carrots with Coriander (page 176)	
Rhubarb and Rose Water Syrup (page 227)	

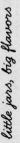

little jars, big flavors

To make this delicious quiche up to two days ahead, cool completely, cover, and store in the refrigerator. On the day of the party, reheat it in a 350° oven for 30 minutes.

CARAMELIZED ONION AND BACON QUICHE

1 (14.1-oz.) package refrigerated piecrusts
3 large sweet onions, sliced (about 1½ lb.)
2 Tbsp. olive oil
½ cup chopped fresh flat-leaf parsley
6 cooked bacon slices, crumbled
2 cups (8 oz.) shredded Gruyère cheese
1½ cups half-and-half
4 large eggs
½ tsp. salt
¼ tsp. freshly ground pepper
¼ tsp. ground nutmeg

1. Preheat oven to 425°. Unroll piecrusts; stack on a lightly greased surface. Roll stacked piecrusts into a 12-inch circle. Fit piecrust into a 10-inch deep-dish tart pan with removable bottom; press into fluted edges. Trim off excess piecrust along edges. Line piecrust with aluminum foil or parchment paper, and fill with pie weights or dried beans. Place pan on a foil-lined baking sheet. Bake 12 minutes. Remove weights and foil, and bake 8 more minutes. Cool completely on baking sheet on a wire rack (about 15 minutes). Reduce oven temperature to 350°.

2. Meanwhile, cook onions in hot oil in a large skillet over medium-high heat, stirring often, 15 to 20 minutes or until onions are caramel colored. Remove from heat, and stir in parsley and bacon. Place half of onion mixture in tart shell, and top with half of cheese; repeat with remaining onion mixture and cheese.

3. Whisk together half-and-half and next 4 ingredients; pour over cheese.

4. Bake at 350° for 40 to 45 minutes or until set. Cool on baking sheet on a wire rack 15 minutes before serving.

The tasty little cakes at the base of this scrumptious dessert can be made a day ahead. So can the strawberry mixture, as long as you chill it. Wait to whip the cream, though, and don't assemble the shortcakes until you're nearly ready to serve them.

STRAWBERRY SHORTCAKES

2 (16-oz.) containers fresh strawberries, quartered
¾ cup sugar, divided
¼ tsp. almond extract (optional)
1 cup whipping cream
2 Tbsp. sugar

2¾ cups all-purpose flour
4 tsp. baking powder
¾ cup cold butter, cut up
2 large eggs, lightly beaten
1 (8-oz.) container sour cream
1 tsp. vanilla extract
Fresh mint sprigs

makes: 8 servings

hands-on time: 25 min.

total time: 3 hours

1. Combine strawberries, ½ cup sugar, and, if desired, almond extract. Cover berry mixture, and let stand 2 hours.

2. Beat whipping cream at medium speed with an electric mixer until foamy; gradually add 2 Tbsp. sugar, beating until soft peaks form. Cover and chill up to 2 hours.

3. Preheat oven to 450°. Combine flour, remaining ¼ cup sugar, and baking powder in a large bowl; cut butter into flour mixture with a pastry blender or two forks until crumbly. Whisk together eggs, sour cream, and vanilla until blended; add to flour mixture, stirring just until dry ingredients are moistened. Drop dough by lightly greased ⅓ cupfuls onto a lightly greased baking sheet. (Coat cup with vegetable cooking spray after each drop.) Bake at 450° for 12 to 15 minutes or until golden. Cool completely (about 20 minutes).

4. Split shortcakes in half horizontally. Spoon about ½ cup berry mixture onto each shortcake bottom; top each with a rounded Tbsp. chilled whipped cream, and cover with tops. Serve with remaining whipped cream, and top with fresh mint sprigs.

SUMMER

Putting-Up Party

WHAT TO PUT UP*

Mixed Berry Jam (page 33)

––––––––

Blackberry-Black Pepper Spread
(page 64)

––––––––

Microwave Nectarine-Ginger
Preserves (page 89)

––––––––

Peach-Bourbon Jam (page 45)

––––––––

Peach-Plum Freezer Jam (page 204)

––––––––

Quick Confetti Pickles (page 146)

––––––––

Pickled Okra (page 164)

––––––––

Basil-Pecan Freezer Pesto (page 216)

*When tomatoes are at their peak, you might
want to devote an entire day to Mediterranean-
Style Tomatoes (page 190), Chunky Marinara
Sauce with Red Wine (page 192), Heirloom
Tomato Chutney (page 187), and Microwave
Tomato-Peach Preserves (page 92). Your pantry
and pocketbook will thank you the rest of the year.

WHAT TO SERVE

Fresh Basil Lemonade
(next page)

––––––––

Meat and cheese platter
with baguette slices

––––––––

Tomato-Cucumber Salad
(next page)

––––––––

Blackberry-Lemon Squares
(page 124)

Steeping lemon zest and fresh herbs in the simple syrup at the base of this drink gives it a little something extra.

FRESH BASIL LEMONADE

½   cup water
1½ cups sugar
1   Tbsp. lemon zest
    (about 2 lemons)

3   (4-inch) basil sprigs
1½ cups fresh lemon juice
    (about 13 lemons)
7   cups ice water

1. Bring ½ cup water to a boil in a medium saucepan. Stir in sugar and lemon zest, stirring until sugar is dissolved; remove from heat. Bruise basil sprigs with the back of a knife; stir into mixture, cover, and steep 10 minutes.

2. Remove and discard herb sprigs. Pour mixture into a pitcher. Stir in lemon juice and ice water. Serve over ice.

makes: 2½ qt.

hands-on time: 5 min.

total time: 20 min.

No Southern spread is complete without this simple summery salad. You can use halved grape or cherry tomatoes in place of the vine-ripened tomatoes.

TOMATO-CUCUMBER SALAD

2   seedless cucumbers, sliced
1   small onion, thinly sliced
4   cups small, vine-ripened
    tomatoes, cut into quarters
½   cup olive oil-and-vinegar
    dressing

1   tsp. lemon zest
2   Tbsp. lemon juice
Salt and pepper to taste

1. Stir together cucumber, onion, and tomatoes. Add oil-and-vinegar dressing, lemon zest, lemon juice, and salt and pepper to taste. Toss to coat.

makes: 8 servings

hands-on time: 10 min.

total time: 10 min.

little jars, big flavors

BLACKBERRY-LEMON SQUARES

makes: 2 dozen

———

hands-on time: 30 min.

———

total time: 2 hours, 25 min.

2¼ cups all-purpose flour, divided
½ cup powdered sugar
1 cup cold butter, cut into pieces
4 large eggs
2 cups granulated sugar, divided
2 tsp. lemon zest
½ cup fresh lemon juice
1 tsp. baking powder
¼ tsp. salt
2 cups fresh blackberries
Powdered sugar

NOTE: The fresh blackberry mixture floats to the top of the lemony base, adding brilliant color to these luscious two-tone fruit bars. You can reserve the blackberry solids and stir them into yogurt, lemonade, or mojitos for added flavor and color.

1. Preheat oven to 350°. Line bottom and sides of a 13- x 9-inch pan with heavy-duty aluminum foil, allowing 2 to 3 inches to extend over sides; lightly grease foil.

2. Pulse 2 cups flour, ½ cup powdered sugar, and 1 cup butter in a food processor 5 to 6 times or until mixture is crumbly. Press mixture onto bottom of prepared pan. Bake at 350° on lower oven rack one-third up from bottom of oven 25 minutes or just until golden brown.

3. Whisk together eggs, 1½ cups sugar, lemon zest, and lemon juice in a large bowl until blended. Combine baking powder, salt, and remaining ¼ cup flour; whisk into egg mixture until blended. Pour lemon mixture into prepared crust.

4. Pulse 2 cups blackberries and remaining ½ cup granulated sugar in a food processor 3 to 4 times or until blended. Transfer mixture to a small saucepan. Cook over medium-low heat, stirring often, 5 to 6 minutes or until thoroughly heated. Pour through a fine wire-mesh strainer into a bowl, gently pressing blackberry mixture with back of a spoon; discard solids. Drizzle blackberry syrup over lemon mixture in pan.

5. Bake at 350° on middle oven rack 30 to 35 minutes or until filling is set. Let cool in pan on a wire rack 30 minutes. Lift from pan onto wire rack, using foil sides as handles, and let cool 30 minutes or until completely cool. Remove foil, and cut into 24 (2-inch) squares; sprinkle with powdered sugar.

little jars, big flavors

FALL

Putting-Up Party

little jars, big flavors

Here's a smoky spin on a classic sub. Pick up sliced pork from your favorite barbecue restaurant. Assemble, press, and chill the big sandwich the day before. Heat and cut into individual portions the day of the party.

SOUTHERN-STYLE CUBANS

¾ cup mayonnaise

2 Tbsp. Creole mustard

2 Tbsp. sweet-hot pickle relish

1 canned chipotle pepper in adobo sauce, chopped

1 Tbsp. chopped fresh flat-leaf parsley

½ tsp. lemon zest

2 tsp. fresh lemon juice

⅛ tsp. salt

⅛ tsp. pepper

1 (12-oz.) French bread loaf

1 lb. sliced barbecued pork without sauce

4 (1-oz.) provolone cheese slices

1 cup sweet-hot pickle slices or ½ cup Hot-and-Sweet Freezer Pickle Relish (page 214)

1. Stir together mayonnaise and next 8 ingredients in a small bowl.

2. Cut French bread loaf in half horizontally; scoop out soft bread from center of each half, leaving a ½-inch-thick shell to make filling the sandwich easier. (Reserve soft bread for another use.) Spread inside of bread shells with mayonnaise mixture. Layer bottom shell with barbecued pork, provolone cheese slices, and sweet-hot pickle slices. Top with remaining bread shell. Flatten sandwich slightly; cut in half crosswise. Wrap halves tightly in plastic wrap; set on a baking sheet, and chill under a weighted baking sheet 4 to 12 hours.

3. Remove plastic wrap. Cook sandwich halves in a hot lightly greased cast-iron skillet or panini press until bread is toasted and cheese is melted (about 5 minutes per side). Cut each half crosswise into 3 or 4 smaller sandwiches.

The sweet and musky flavor of Scuppernong grapes is the perfect foil for fall flavors such as blue cheese and walnuts. Not to worry, though: You can use prepared jelly for the glaze if you haven't gotten around to canning your own yet.

PEAR-BLUE CHEESE TART

1 (17.3-oz.) package frozen puff pastry sheets, thawed

1 large egg

⅓ cup Scuppernong Jelly (page 54) or prepared grape or apple jelly, divided

1 firm, ripe Barlett pear, peeled and thinly sliced

½ cup (2 oz.) crumbled blue cheese

½ cup chopped walnuts

makes: 8 to 10 servings

hands-on time: 12 min.

total time: 40 min.

1. Preheat oven to 400°. Roll 1 pastry sheet into a 12-inch square on a lightly floured surface; place on an ungreased baking sheet. Roll remaining pastry sheet into a 12-inch square. Cut 4 (12- x 1-inch) strips from pastry, reserving remaining pastry for another use.

2. Whisk together egg and 1 Tbsp. water. Brush edges of pastry square with egg mixture. Place dough strips along outer edges of pastry square, pressing gently to form a border. Brush border with egg mixture. Prick bottom of tart with a fork. Bake at 400° for 10 minutes or until lightly browned.

3. Place jelly in a microwave-safe bowl. Cover and microwave at HIGH 30 seconds; stir until jelly melts.

4. Arrange pear slices on bottom of dough, overlapping slightly. Brush ¼ cup melted jelly over pear slices. Sprinkle pear with blue cheese and walnuts. Drizzle remaining jelly over top. Bake at 400° for 18 minutes or until crust is browned and pear is crisp-tender. Serve warm.

little jars, big flavors

WINTER

Putting-Up Party

little jars, big flavors

A hot oven makes these sweet potatoes, parsnips, and beets extra sweet. Roast them (separately, so the beets don't stain everything red), and make the dressing up to two days ahead. On party day, simply toss them with dressing, and serve them over arugula.

ROASTED ROOT VEGETABLE SALAD

2	large sweet potatoes (about 1½ lb.)
4	large parsnips (about 1 lb.)
6	medium beets (about 1½ lb.)
3	Tbsp. olive oil, divided
1¾	tsp. salt, divided
1	tsp. pepper, divided
½	cup bottled olive oil-and-vinegar dressing
1	Tbsp. chopped fresh parsley
1	Tbsp. refrigerated horseradish
1	tsp. Dijon mustard
	Fresh arugula

makes: 6 to 8 servings

hands-on time: 30 min.

total time: 1 hour, 30 min.

1. Preheat oven to 400°. Peel sweet potatoes, and cut into ¾-inch cubes. Peel parsnips, and cut into ½-inch slices. Peel beets, and cut into ½-inch-thick wedges.

2. Toss sweet potatoes and parsnips with 2 Tbsp. olive oil in a large bowl; place in a single layer in a lightly greased 15- x 10-inch jelly-roll pan. Sprinkle with 1¼ tsp. salt and ½ tsp. pepper.

3. Toss beets with remaining 1 Tbsp. olive oil; arrange beets in a single layer on a separate aluminum foil-lined 15- x 10-inch jelly-roll pan. Sprinkle with remaining ½ tsp. salt and ½ tsp. pepper.

4. Bake at 400° for 40 to 45 minutes or just until tender. Let cool completely (about 20 minutes).

5. Meanwhile, whisk together dressing and next 3 ingredients. Place vegetables in a large bowl, and drizzle with desired amount of dressing; toss gently to coat. Serve at room temperature or chilled over arugula with any remaining dressing.

little jars, big flavors

To make these casual, three-bite sandwiches ahead, prepare as directed through Step 3, and freeze up to a month. Take out as much as you need for the party a day ahead, thaw it overnight in the refrigerator, and bake as directed in Step 4 on party day.

HOT ROAST BEEF PARTY SANDWICHES

makes: 12 to 16 servings

hands-on time: 26 min.

total time: 56 min.

½ cup finely chopped walnuts
2 (9¼-oz.) packages dinner rolls
⅔ cup peach preserves
½ cup mustard-mayonnaise blend
¾ lb. thinly sliced deli roast beef, chopped
½ lb. thinly sliced Havarti cheese
Salt and pepper (optional)

1. Preheat oven to 325°.

2. Heat walnuts in a small nonstick skillet over medium-low heat, stirring often, 5 to 6 minutes or until lightly toasted and fragrant.

3. Remove rolls from packages. (Do not separate rolls.) Cut rolls in half horizontally, creating 1 top and 1 bottom per package. Spread preserves on cut sides of top of rolls; sprinkle with walnuts. Spread mustard-mayonnaise blend on cut sides of bottom of rolls; top with roast beef and cheese. Sprinkle with salt and pepper, if desired. Cover with top halves of rolls, preserves sides down, and wrap in aluminum foil.

4. Bake at 325° for 30 minutes or until cheese is melted. Slice into individual sandwiches. Serve immediately.

Strawberry and peach jams make beautiful jewel-colored fillings for these nutty, buttery cookies, but you can use any jam or preserves you like.

THUMBPRINT COOKIES

1	cup butter, softened		¼	tsp. salt
¾	cup sugar		1¼	cups finely chopped pecans
2	large eggs, separated		¼	cup strawberry jam
1	tsp. almond extract		¼	cup peach jam
2	cups all-purpose flour			

1. Beat butter at medium speed with an electric mixer until creamy; gradually add sugar, beating well. Add egg yolks and almond extract, beating until blended.

2. Combine flour and salt; add to butter mixture, beating at low speed until blended. Cover and chill dough 1 hour.

3. Preheat oven to 350°. Shape dough into 1-inch balls. Lightly beat egg whites. Dip each dough ball in egg white; roll in pecans. Place 2 inches apart on ungreased baking sheets. Press thumb in each dough ball to make an indentation.

4. Bake at 350° for 15 minutes. Cool 1 minute on baking sheets, and remove to wire racks to cool completely. Press centers again with thumb while cookies are still warm; fill center of each cookie with jam.

makes: 3½ dozen for the table

hands-on time: 35 min.

total time: 2 hours, 5 min.

little jars, big flavors

SHARING WHAT YOU'VE BOTTLED AND CANNED

LABELS When the putting-up party is over, you'll have jars aplenty to enjoy with your family or to share with others. I like to save several for thank-you and hostess gifts. Handmade food takes time, one of life's most precious commodities, which makes each jar a thoughtful gift in its own right, or a smart way to add personality to a gift basket.

Whether they're going to Grandma's house or to your pantry, jars should be labeled as soon as they're cool to avoid later confusion. (Mint Jelly and Tart Basil Jelly look an awful lot alike. So too, to the untrained eye, do Strawberry-Basil Jam and Strawberry-Port

Jam.) At a minimum, each label should include the recipe title and the date prepared. A use-by date and the name of the person who made the preserves are also nice when they're going to someone else's house.

Place labels on the sides of the jars or on top of the lids. If the label's only temporary, and you're planning something fancier later, stick it on the bottom of the jar to avoid gunking up the sides.

little jars, big flavors

You can use the simple labels that are included with some canning jars, plain old masking tape, or even a permanent marker on the top of the lid to identify what's in the jar. Practical and pretty needn't be mutually exclusive. Neat label options abound. Here are a few I like:

Avery Labels with Downloadable Patterns: These plain self-adhesive labels come in printer-sized sheets and have a smooth paper backing that can be removed easily. They can be customized on a home laser or inkjet printer with downloadable designs. Etsy.com and other online sites offer a wide selection of fun patterns, from retro to modern, country to chic.

Gummed Labels: Widely available in office and art supply stores, these are plain or preprinted with a decorative border. You can use a stamp and inkpad to decorate your own. If you're hand-lettering them, be sure to use permanent marker or nonsmudging ink.

Chalkboard Labels: These attractive vinyl labels have a gummed backing and chalkboard-like surface that makes them reusable. Just write on them with chalk or a white nail pencil, wipe with a moist cloth or towel, and write on them again. If you're worried about the label getting wet and washing off, you can also use a white ink pen for a more permanent label.

GIFT TAGS & OTHER DECORATIONS A few years ago, I received a jar of delicious marmalade during the holidays and unfortunately lost the gift tag in the hustle and bustle of the season. I didn't know who to thank—or how soon to use it. That's why I find tied-on tags less than ideal for conveying the recipe name, the date prepared, and the name of the cook. I think that belongs on the jar.

Still, a gift tag has its advantages. It can gussy up the jar and add extra information (such as holiday wishes) for the recipient. Gift tags are excellent places to put short recipes or practical suggestions for how to use what's in the jar.

Look for ready-made tags online and in office supply or arts and crafts stores, or make your own with squares of scrapbooking paper or recycled cardstock. Use a hole puncher to make a clean hole, and tie on tags with ribbon or string. If you want to go one further, accessorize with any of the following:

Cloth Caps: Gingham, burlap, or simple cloth can be placed over the lid and tied on with string or secured with the metal band for a sweet presentation. To make a cloth cover, cut a square or circle of fabric long enough to skirt the top of the jar. Be sure to choose fabric that will complement the color of your preserved goods. Use pinking shears to minimize fraying. Lay the cloth over the lid, and secure with the metal band or twine.

Paper: Wax paper, tissue paper, or a combination of both also can pretty up a jar. Unscrew the lid ring. Cut circles of paper 2 inches larger in diameter than the ring. Place the paper on top of the sealed lid, and screw the lid ring over the paper to secure it.

Add-ons: Herb sprigs, cinnamon sticks, and star anise are lovely natural additions to little jars. You can attach them with twine, string, or ribbon. To avoid confusion, only decorate with ingredients that are actually used in the preserved recipe. Small spoons, spreaders, or buttons also make decorative tie-ons.

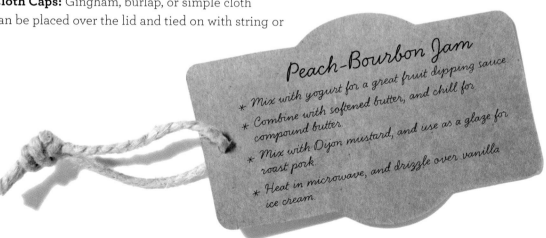

Peach-Bourbon Jam

* Mix with yogurt for a great fruit dipping sauce
* Combine with softened butter, and chill for compound butter.
* Mix with Dijon mustard, and use as a glaze for roast pork.
* Heat in microwave, and drizzle over vanilla ice cream.

PACKING UP

At the end of a putting-up party, the putting-up-your-feet part of the day, when the kitchen is clean, and it's time to say good-bye to your preserving pals, everyone will need to safely, smartly transport their precious cargo home.

It's important to let any hot jars cool before you move them and keep the jars upright until they are fully sealed. A broken jar of hot jelly is a burn, a cut, or both waiting to happen. And jostling any just-pickled item can interfere with its seal. Next-day delivery or pickups may be necessary.

But what to put them in? If you've saved the boxes the jars were sold in, and you have boxes for everyone, you've got it made. But you might need to consider other options. Here are some green suggestions to help with the end-of-party takeaway:

Reduce, reuse, recycle—and rethink! Use old shoeboxes, and wrap the jars in newspaper to prevent them from clanking and possibly cracking.

Reusable wine bags and cartons with dividers are perfect for transporting a half-dozen pint jars.

Handled shopping bags with sturdy bottoms, like those from upscale clothing stores, are excellent for transporting jars. Just be sure to use newspaper or kitchen towels to keep the jars from knocking together or tipping over in the bag.

Inexpensive wicker baskets and hat boxes, available at thrift and craft supply stores, work nicely.

Planning more putting-up parties? Consider investing in vintage-style wire milk bottle carriers. They are sturdy, stylish, and reusable. Look for them online, at flea markets, and in antiques and retro housewares stores.

Even if this sounds daunting now, you're bound to crave seasonal sessions with friends throughout the year after you've gotten one putting-up party under your belt. With the basic gear on hand and a taste for canning in your system, you'll spot opportunities for preserving each season.

Trust me, the more you do it, the more natural it'll seem. Before you know it, you too may be making jelly right along with dinner, turning extra summer squash into pickles instead of compost before you leave on vacation, or calling up friends with a hatched-at-the-market plan for an impromptu "jam" session. Here's wishing you your own breakthrough moment.

• ◆ •

Southern Living contributing editor Virginia Willis is an Atlanta-based food writer, a professionally trained chef, and author of the cookbook *Basic to Brilliant, Y'all: 150 Refined Southern Recipes and Ways to Dress Them Up for Company* (Ten Speed Press, 2011).

little jars, big flavors

PICKLES, RELISHES & SAUCES

These classic spears are crisp, sour, and a sandwich's best friend. Like most pickles, they'll reach their best flavor and texture after three weeks in the jars.

DILL PICKLE SPEARS

4   lb. (3- to 5-inch) pickling cucumbers
10 Tbsp. canning-and-pickling salt, divided
3   cups white vinegar (5% acidity)
2   Tbsp. sugar
1   Tbsp. pickling spice
12 dill sprigs
2   Tbsp. whole mustard seeds

1. Wash cucumbers, and trim any that are longer than 4 inches (so that they'll fit comfortably in the jar). Cut each cucumber lengthwise into quarters. Place spears in a large clean container (such as a 12- to 18-qt. plastic pail or dish basin). Combine 6 Tbsp. salt and 1 gal. water in a large pitcher, stirring until salt dissolves. Pour over cucumbers; cover and let stand at room temperature 24 hours. Drain.

2. Sterilize jars, and prepare lids as described on page 22.

3. While jars are boiling, combine vinegar, next 2 ingredients, remaining ¼ cup salt, and 1 qt. water in a 3-qt. stainless steel saucepan. Bring to a boil.

4. Place 2 dill sprigs and 1 tsp. mustard seeds in each hot jar. Pack jars tightly with cucumber spears. Cover spears with hot pickling liquid, leaving ½-inch headspace. Seal and process jars as described on pages 22–25, processing 10 minutes.

5. Remove jars from water, and let stand, undisturbed, at room temperature 24 hours. To check seals, remove the bands, and press down on the center of each lid. If the lid doesn't move, the jar is sealed. If the lid depresses and pops up again, the jar is not sealed. Store properly sealed jars in a cool, dark place up to 1 year. Refrigerate after opening.

makes: 6 (1-pt.) widemouthed jars for the shelf

hands-on time: 20 min.

total time: 50 min., plus 1 day brining and 3 weeks standing time

NOTE: Pickling cucumbers are small, crisp, unwaxed, and needn't be peeled. Widemouthed jars aren't essential for pickles, but they do make for easier packing.

little jars, big flavors

Try these sweet-and-sour pickles on sandwiches, in deviled eggs, or straight out of the jar.

BREAD-AND-BUTTER PICKLES

4¾ lb. medium cucumbers

4 large onions

1 large green bell pepper, chopped

¼ cup canning-and-pickling salt

2½ cups white vinegar (5% acidity)

2 cups sugar

2 Tbsp. mustard seeds

¾ tsp. ground turmeric

5 whole cloves

1. Scrub cucumbers thoroughly to remove any wax; trim stem and blossom ends, and cut cucumbers crosswise into ¼-inch-thick slices. Cut onions in half, and slice crosswise into ⅛-inch-thick slices. Place cucumber, onion, and bell pepper in a bowl; toss with salt. Cover and let stand 3 hours at room temperature; drain.

2. Sterilize jars, and prepare lids as described on page 22. While jars are boiling, bring vinegar and next 4 ingredients to a boil in an 8-qt. stainless steel or enameled stockpot, stirring just until sugar dissolves. Add drained cucumber mixture, and cook, stirring often, 7 to 10 minutes or until mixture is thoroughly heated and cucumber peels turn dark green.

3. Ladle hot mixture into hot jars, leaving ½-inch headspace. Seal and process jars as described on pages 22–25, processing 10 minutes.

4. Remove jars from water, and let stand, undisturbed, at room temperature 24 hours. To check seals, remove the bands, and press down on the center of each lid. If the lid doesn't move, the jar is sealed. If the lid depresses and pops up again, the jar is not sealed. Store properly sealed jars in a cool, dark place up to 1 year. Refrigerate after opening.

little jars, big flavors

This colorful blend mimics bread-and-butter pickles—sweet, tart, and squeaky-crisp—even though it contains no cucumbers. Use the freshest zucchini and yellow squash you can find, free of blemishes and with no hint of limpness, for the crispiest results.

SQUASH PICKLE MEDLEY

4	large zucchini squash (2½ lb.)
4	large yellow squash (1¼ lb.)
1	(8-oz.) onion, halved vertically and cut crosswise into ¼-inch slices (curved strips)
⅓	cup canning-and-pickling salt

	Ice cubes
2	cups white vinegar (5% acidity)
2	cups sugar
1	tsp. mustard seeds
½	tsp. celery seeds
¼	tsp. ground turmeric

makes: 4 (1-pt.) widemouthed jars for the shelf

hands-on time: 55 min.

total time: 4 hours, 10 min., plus 3 weeks standing time

1. Wash zucchini and yellow squash, and trim stem and blossom ends; cut squash crosswise into ¼-inch slices. Toss squash and onion with salt in a very large bowl. Cover vegetables with ice cubes. Cover and let stand at room temperature 3 hours.

2. Sterilize jars, and prepare lids as described on page 22.

3. While jars are boiling, drain vegetables, but do not rinse, discarding brine and any unmelted ice. Return drained vegetables to bowl. Combine vinegar and next 4 ingredients in a medium stainless steel saucepan. Bring to a boil over medium-high heat.

4. Pack squash and onion mixture tightly into hot jars, leaving ½-inch headspace. Cover vegetables with hot pickling liquid, leaving ½-inch headspace. Seal and process jars as described on pages 22–25, processing 10 minutes.

5. Remove jars from water, and let stand, undisturbed, at room temperature 24 hours. To check seals, remove the bands, and press down on the center of each lid. If the lid doesn't move, the jar is sealed. If the lid depresses and pops up again, the jar is not sealed. Store properly sealed jars in a cool, dark place up to 1 year. Refrigerate after opening.

little jars, big flavors

No time to can? No problem. These refrigerator pickles are easy—and so colorful that you'll want to shingle them on buttered brown bread or put them in a glass bowl just to show them off. Standard radishes will do, but slender, carrotlike icicle radishes from the farmers' market are easier to slice.

QUICK CONFETTI PICKLES

1	English cucumber
1	medium-size yellow squash
4	Tbsp. canning-and-pickling salt, divided
1	long, slender medium carrot
2	pink, purple, or red icicle radishes or 10 standard-size radishes
4	dill sprigs
1	cup cider vinegar (5% acidity)
¼	cup sugar
2	Tbsp. lemon juice
1	tsp. dill seeds

makes: 2 (1-pt.) jars for the fridge

hands-on time: 30 min.

total time: 1 hour, plus 1 day standing time

1. Wash vegetables. Score cucumber and squash lengthwise with a fork, leaving furrows in the peel on all sides. (This makes scalloped edges when vegetables are sliced.) Trim stem and blossom ends of cucumber and squash; cut into ⅛-inch slices. Place in a colander in sink; sprinkle with 2 Tbsp. salt, and toss gently. Let drain 30 minutes.

2. Meanwhile, peel carrot, and cut carrot and radishes into ⅛-inch-thick slices. Toss together with drained cucumber and squash.

3. Place 2 dill sprigs in each of 2 clean (1-pt.) jars or nonreactive containers with lids. Pack vegetables in jars, leaving ½-inch headspace.

4. Bring vinegar, next 3 ingredients, remaining 2 Tbsp. salt, and 2 cups water to a boil in a 1½-qt. stainless steel saucepan over medium-high heat, stirring until sugar and salt dissolve. Pour hot vinegar mixture over vegetables to cover. Apply lids. Chill 24 hours before serving. Store in refrigerator up to 3 weeks.

If you like things hot, you'll love these fiery pickles. They're ideal as a final atomic flourish on tacos, nachos, and huevos rancheros. If you prefer milder pickled peppers, cut off the stem ends, and scoop or tap out some of the seeds before slicing the peppers.

PICKLED JALAPEÑO SLICES

¾ lb. green jalapeño peppers
¼ lb. red jalapeño peppers
1½ cups white vinegar (5% acidity)

1 tsp. canning-and-pickling salt
4 large garlic cloves, halved
4 bay leaves

1. Sterilize jars, and prepare lids as described on page 22.

2. While jars are boiling, put on gloves, and cut peppers into ¼-inch slices, discarding stem ends. Combine vinegar, salt, and 1½ cups water in a medium stainless steel saucepan; bring to a boil.

3. Place 2 garlic halves and 1 bay leaf in each hot jar. Pack jars tightly with peppers, leaving ½-inch headspace. Cover peppers with hot pickling liquid, leaving ½-inch headspace. Seal and process jars as described on pages 22–25, processing 10 minutes.

4. Remove jars from water, and let stand, undisturbed, at room temperature 24 hours. To check seals, remove the bands, and press down on the center of each lid. If the lid doesn't move, the jar is sealed. If the lid depresses and pops up again, the jar is not sealed. Store properly sealed jars in a cool, dark place up to 1 year. Refrigerate after opening.

makes: 4 (½-pt.) jars
for the shelf

hands-on time: 25 min.

total time: 45 min.,
plus 3 weeks standing time

little jars, big flavors

Try these crunchy cloves in dirty martinis and anywhere you'd use fresh garlic. The garlic is mellowed and crisped by pickling and enhanced by hot peppers, and the hit of vinegar brightens any savory dish.

PICKLED GARLIC WITH CHILES

1½	cups white vinegar (5% acidity)	8	whole black peppercorns
1	tsp. canning-and-pickling salt	2	cups peeled garlic cloves
½	tsp. sugar	4	small bay leaves
3	small dried chile peppers, halved		

1. Sterilize jars, and prepare lids as described on page 22.

2. While jars are boiling, combine first 5 ingredients in a large stainless steel saucepan; bring to a boil. Add garlic; bring to a boil, and boil 4 minutes. Remove from heat.

3. Place 1 bay leaf in each hot jar. Using a slotted spoon, divide garlic and halved chiles (discard remaining halved chile) evenly among hot jars, packing tightly and leaving ¼-inch headspace; cover with hot pickling liquid, leaving ¼-inch headspace. Seal and process jars as described on pages 22–25, processing 10 minutes.

4. Remove jars from water, and let stand, undisturbed, at room temperature 24 hours. To check seals, remove the bands, and press down on the center of each lid. If the lid doesn't move, the jar is sealed. If the lid depresses and pops up again, the jar is not sealed. Store properly sealed jars in a cool, dark place up to 1 year. Refrigerate after opening.

This recipe works with red beets, too, but golden beets are less likely to stain your fingers or your apron.

PICKLED GOLDEN BEETS

3¾ lb. (3-inch-diameter) golden beets

2½ cups white vinegar (5% acidity)

1¼ cups sugar

1 tsp. canning-and-pickling salt

1 (3-inch) cinnamon stick

8 whole cloves

2 (2- to 2½-inch-diameter) onions, thinly sliced

makes: 4 (1-pt.) widemouthed jars for the shelf

hands-on time: 45 min.

total time: 1 hour, 55 min., plus 3 weeks standing time

1. Trim beets, leaving 1 inch of stem, and scrub. Bring beets to a boil in water to cover in a medium saucepan; reduce heat, and simmer 25 to 30 minutes or until tender. Drain, rinse, and cool slightly. Trim off roots and stems; peel beets. Cut beets in half vertically; cut halves into ¼-inch-thick slices to measure 6 cups.

2. Sterilize jars, and prepare lids as described on page 22.

3. While jars are boiling, stir together vinegar, next 4 ingredients, and 1¼ cups water in a stainless steel or enameled 8-qt. Dutch oven. Bring mixture to a boil. Add beets and onions; reduce heat, and simmer 5 minutes. Remove and discard spices.

4. Using a slotted spoon, divide beets and onions evenly among hot jars, leaving ½-inch headspace. Cover beet mixture with hot pickling liquid, leaving ½-inch headspace. Seal and process jars as described on pages 22–25, processing 30 minutes.

5. Remove jars from water, and let stand, undisturbed, at room temperature 24 hours. To check seals, remove the bands, and press down on the center of each lid. If the lid doesn't move, the jar is sealed. If the lid depresses and pops up again, the jar is not sealed. Store properly sealed jars in a cool, dark place up to 1 year. Refrigerate after opening.

little jars, big flavors

Crushed red pepper gives these beans a kick. A mix of green and yellow beans makes for a pretty jar.

PICKLED DILLED BEANS

3	lb. fresh green or yellow beans (5 to 6 inches long)	1½	tsp. dried crushed red pepper
6	cups white vinegar (5% acidity)	12	fresh dill sprigs
⅔	cup canning-and-pickling salt	6	garlic cloves, peeled

1. Sterilize jars, and prepare lids as described on page 22.

2. While jars are boiling, wash beans, trim stem ends, and cut into 4-inch lengths. Combine vinegar, salt, crushed red pepper, and 2 cups water in a 3-qt. stainless steel saucepan. Bring to a boil.

3. Place 2 dill sprigs and 1 garlic clove in each hot jar. Pack whole beans tightly in jars. Cover with hot pickling liquid, leaving ½-inch headspace. Seal and process jars as described on pages 22–25, processing 5 minutes.

4. Remove jars from water, and let stand, undisturbed, at room temperature 24 hours. To check seals, remove the bands, and press down on the center of each lid. If the lid doesn't move, the jar is sealed. If the lid depresses and pops up again, the jar is not sealed. Store properly sealed jars in a cool, dark place up to 1 year. Refrigerate after opening.

makes: 6 (1-pt.) widemouthed jars for the shelf

hands-on time: 40 min.

total time: 55 min., plus 3 weeks standing time

Use these crisp, tart onions as sandwich toppers, martini garnishes, or interesting additions to meat-and-cheese platters.

PICKLED PEARL ONIONS

22 (10-oz.) packages fresh pearl onions	1 tsp. canning-and-pickling salt
2¾ cups white vinegar (5% acidity)	3¾ tsp. mustard seeds
1 cup sugar	1½ tsp. celery seeds
	12 whole cloves

1. Place onions a large pot of boiling water 30 seconds; drain. Plunge into ice water to stop the cooking process; drain. Trim and discard ends of each onion, and slip off skins.

2. Sterilize jars, and prepare lids as described on page 22.

3. While jars are boiling, bring vinegar, sugar, salt, and ½ cup water to a boil in a 6-qt. stainless steel or enameled Dutch oven over high heat. Boil 3 minutes, stirring occasionally. Add peeled onions, and return to a boil. Reduce heat, and simmer 4 minutes or until onions are almost tender.

4. Place 1¼ tsp. mustard seeds, ½ tsp. celery seeds, and 4 cloves in each hot jar. Pack onions tightly in jars, leaving ½-inch headspace. Cover onions with hot pickling liquid, leaving ½-inch headspace. Seal and process jars as described on pages 22–25, processing 10 minutes.

5. Remove jars from water, and let stand, undisturbed, at room temperature 24 hours. To check seals, remove the bands, and press down on the center of each lid. If the lid doesn't move, the jar is sealed. If the lid depresses and pops up again, the jar is not sealed. Store properly sealed jars in a cool, dark place up to 1 year. Refrigerate after opening.

makes: 3 (½-pt.) jars for the shelf

hands-on time: 1 hour

total time: 1 hour, 11 min., plus 3 weeks standing time

little jars, big flavors

These juicy white salad turnips shrink considerably during processing, so pack them tightly into the jars, fitting the wedges together like puzzle pieces. Save some of the finished pickles for a Vietnamese-style sandwich (recipe on page 160).

PICKLED JAPANESE TURNIPS WITH SHISO

2½ lb. hakurei turnips
4 cups white vinegar (5% acidity)
¼ cup canning-and-pickling salt
¼ cup sugar
6 fresh red or green shiso leaves
3 serrano peppers
3 garlic cloves

1. Sterilize jars, and prepare lids as described on page 22.

2. While jars are boiling, scrub turnips thoroughly, and remove any blemishes; trim off green tops. Cut turnips into 1-inch wedges. Bring vinegar, salt, sugar, and ½ cup water to a boil in a 3-qt. stainless steel saucepan over medium heat, stirring to dissolve sugar and salt.

3. Place 2 shiso leaves, 1 serrano pepper, and 1 garlic clove in each hot jar. Pack turnips tightly in jars, leaving ½-inch headspace. Cover turnips with hot pickling liquid, leaving ½-inch headspace.

4. Seal and process jars as described on pages 22–25, processing 15 minutes.

5. Remove jars from water, and let stand, undisturbed, at room temperature 24 hours. To check seals, remove the bands, and press down on the center of each lid. If the lid doesn't move, the jar is sealed. If the lid depresses and pops up again, the jar is not sealed. Store properly sealed jars in a cool, dark place up to 1 year. Refrigerate after opening.

makes: 3 (1-pt.) jars for the shelf

hands-on time: 30 min.

total time: 45 min., plus 3 weeks standing time

NOTE: Look for hakurei turnips at farmers' markets, and lemony shiso leaves at Asian markets. Green and red leaves work equally well, but the red shiso lends a slight pink color to the brine and the turnips.

BÁNH MÌ WITH PICKLED JAPANESE TURNIPS

(pictured on page 159)

(pictured on page 159)

makes: 4 servings for the table

———

hands-on time: 20 min.

———

total time: 25 min.

NOTE: Omit the carrots from this Vietnamese-style sandwich, and substitute Asian-Style Carrot and Daikon Pickles (page 163) and their juice for the pickled turnips and juice if you prefer.

1 cup shredded carrots

1 cup Pickled Japanese Turnips with Shiso (page 158), coarsely chopped

¼ cup juice from Pickled Japanese Turnips with Shiso

¼ cup sugar

¼ tsp. salt

¼ lb. liverwurst

¼ cup mayonnaise

½ tsp. freshly ground pepper

8 thin boneless pork loin cutlets (1 lb.)

½ tsp. Chinese five spice

1 Tbsp. dark sesame oil, divided

2 Tbsp. hoisin sauce

2 Tbsp. soy sauce

½ tsp. Asian chili-garlic sauce

2 (8.5-oz.) French bread baguettes (about 16 inches long)

½ cup loosely packed cilantro sprigs

1 cup thinly sliced English cucumber

1 jalapeño pepper, thinly sliced

4 green leaf lettuce leaves (optional)

1. Preheat oven to 350°. Toss together first 5 ingredients in a small bowl. Process liverwurst, mayonnaise, and freshly ground pepper in a food processor until smooth.

2. Sprinkle pork evenly with Chinese five spice. Cook 4 pork cutlets in 1 tsp. hot sesame oil in a large nonstick skillet over medium-high heat 2 minutes on each side or until golden brown. Repeat with remaining pork and 1 tsp. oil.

3. Stir together remaining 1 tsp. sesame oil, hoisin sauce, soy sauce, and chili-garlic sauce in a shallow dish. Add cooked pork to sauce, turning to coat.

4. Place baguettes on oven rack, and bake at 350° for 4 minutes or until warm and crisp. Cut each baguette in half crosswise; cut bread halves lengthwise. Spread liverwurst mixture on cut sides of bread. Place turnip mixture, cilantro, cucumber slices, pork cutlets, jalapeño slices, and lettuce on bottom halves of bread; cover with top halves of bread.

little jars, big flavors

These refrigerator pickles are a fun way to introduce newbies to kohlrabi, the peppery vegetable that resembles an alien. You can use green kohlrabi as well, but using purple kohlrabi and leaving the skin on yields pickles that are faintly pink.

QUICK KOHLRABI PICKLES

2   small (3-inch-diameter) purple kohlrabi
4   dill sprigs
¼   cup canning-and-pickling salt

¼   cup sugar
1   cup cider vinegar (5% acidity)
2   Tbsp. lemon juice
1   tsp. dill seeds

makes: 2 (1-pt.) jars for the fridge

hands-on time: 20 min.

total time: 30 min., plus 1 day standing time

1. Wash kohlrabi; trim off and discard root end, stems, leaves, and any surface blemishes. Quarter kohlrabi. Cut quarters into ⅛-inch slices using a V-slicer or mandoline. Stack slices, and cut into ⅛-inch-thick julienne strips using a mandoline or knife.

2. Place 2 dill sprigs in each of 2 clean (1-pt.) jars or nonreactive containers with lids. Tightly pack kohlrabi in jars, leaving ½-inch headspace.

3. Bring remaining ingredients and 2 cups water to boil in a 1½-qt. stainless steel saucepan over medium-high heat, stirring until sugar and salt dissolve. Pour hot vinegar mixture over vegetables to cover. Apply lids. Chill 24 hours before serving. Store in refrigerator up to 3 weeks.

Large carrots (easier to julienne with a mandoline) work best for this recipe. Use two chiles per jar if you prefer spicier pickles.

ASIAN-STYLE CARROT AND DAIKON PICKLES

1	lb. large carrots
1	lb. daikon radishes
2	cups white vinegar (5% acidity)
1	cup sugar
¼	cup canning-and-pickling salt
1	(1-inch) piece fresh ginger, peeled and thinly sliced
8	garlic cloves
4	Tbsp. coriander seeds
4 to 8	small dried red chiles (such as bird's beak peppers or pequin chiles)

makes: 4 (1-pt.) jars for the shelf

hands-on time: 30 min.

total time: 30 min., plus 3 weeks standing time

1. Sterilize jars, and prepare lids as described on page 22.

2. While jars are boiling, peel carrots and radishes, and cut into ⅛-inch-thick julienne strips using a mandoline or knife.

3. Bring 2 cups water, vinegar, sugar, salt, ginger, and garlic to a boil in a 6-qt. stainless steel or enameled Dutch oven.

4. Place 1 Tbsp. coriander seeds, 1 to 2 chiles, 2 garlic cloves, and one-fourth of the ginger slices in each hot jar. Pack carrots and radishes tightly in jars, leaving ½-inch headspace. Cover vegetables with hot pickling liquid, leaving ½-inch headspace. Seal and process jars as described on pages 22–25, processing 5 minutes.

5. Remove jars from water, and let stand, undisturbed, at room temperature 24 hours. To check seals, remove the bands, and press down on the center of each lid. If the lid doesn't move, the jar is sealed. If the lid depresses and pops up again, the jar is not sealed. Store properly sealed jars in a cool, dark place up to 1 year. Refrigerate after opening.

little jars, big flavors

Okra shrink and float when pickled. To get the most in each jar, pack one layer of okra with stem ends down and tips up and another layer with stem ends up and tips down, interlacing the tips in the middle of the jar.

PICKLED OKRA

3   lb. (2½- to 3-inch) okra pods
3   cups white vinegar (5% acidity)
⅓   cup canning-and-pickling salt
2   tsp. dill seeds

5   garlic cloves, peeled
3   small fresh hot red peppers, halved (optional)

1. Sterilize jars, and prepare lids as described on page 22.

2. While jars are boiling, wash okra and trim stems, leaving caps intact. Combine vinegar, salt, dill seeds, and 3 cups water in large stainless steel saucepan. Bring to a boil.

3. Place 1 garlic clove and, if desired, 1 hot pepper half in each hot jar. Pack okra pods tightly in jars, placing some stem end down and some stem end up and leaving ½-inch headspace. Cover okra with hot pickling liquid, leaving ½-inch headspace.

4. Seal and process jars as described on pages 22–25, processing 10 minutes.

5. Remove jars from water, and let stand, undisturbed, at room temperature 24 hours. To check seals, remove the bands, and press down on the center of each lid. If the lid doesn't move, the jar is sealed. If the lid depresses and pops up again, the jar is not sealed. Store properly sealed jars in a cool, dark place up to 1 year. Refrigerate after opening.

This medley of bell peppers and red onion is the perfect accompaniment to a sandwich or an appetizer tray.

PICKLED PEPPERS & ONIONS

1   cup (¼-inch-thick) red onion slices

2   cups white vinegar (5% acidity)

¾   cup sugar

¼   cup canning-and-pickling salt

1   tsp. dried crushed red pepper

1   medium red bell pepper, cut into ¼-inch-thick strips

1   medium yellow bell pepper, cut into ¼-inch-thick strips

1   large green bell pepper, cut into ¼-inch-thick strips

makes: 3 (1-pt.) jars for the shelf

hands-on time: 58 min.

total time: 1 hour, 8 min., plus 3 weeks standing time

1. Sterilize jars, and prepare lids as described on page 22.

2. While jars are boiling, soak onion slices in ice water 10 minutes. Bring vinegar, next 3 ingredients, and 2 cups water to a boil in a 1-qt. stainless steel saucepan over medium-high heat, stirring until sugar dissolves.

3. Drain onion slices; pat dry. Toss together onions and bell peppers. Pack vegetables tightly in hot jars, leaving ½-inch headspace. Cover vegetables with hot pickling liquid, leaving ½-inch headspace.

4. Seal and process jars as described on pages 22–25, processing 5 minutes.

5. Remove jars from water, and let stand, undisturbed, at room temperature 24 hours. To check seals, remove the bands, and press down on the center of each lid. If the lid doesn't move, the jar is sealed. If the lid depresses and pops up again, the jar is not sealed. Store properly sealed jars in a cool, dark place up to 1 year. Refrigerate after opening.

You need to trim the asparagus to fit your jars, but you needn't discard the tender trimmings. Chop them evenly, blanch or sauté, and add to spring pasta or egg dishes.

PICKLED ASPARAGUS

makes: 3 (1-pt.)
widemouthed jars for the shelf

———

hands-on time: 42 min.

———

total time: 42 min.,
plus 3 weeks standing time

2½ cups white vinegar (5% acidity)
⅓ cup sugar
¼ cup canning-and-pickling salt
2 tsp. dried crushed red pepper
1 tsp. pickling spice

3¼ lb. fresh asparagus
(about 3 large bunches)
6 dill sprigs
3 garlic cloves

1. Sterilize jars, and prepare lids as described on page 22.

2. While jars are boiling, bring 2 cups water, vinegar, and next 4 ingredients to a boil in a 3-qt. stainless steel saucepan over medium-high heat, stirring until sugar and salt dissolve.

3. Rinse asparagus; snap off and discard tough ends of asparagus. Trim spears to 4-inch lengths (to fit jars). Place 2 dill sprigs and 1 garlic clove in each hot jar. Tightly pack asparagus, cut ends down, in jars, leaving ½-inch headspace. Cover with hot pickling liquid, leaving ½-inch headspace.

4. Seal and process jars as described on pages 22–25, processing 10 minutes.

5. Remove jars from water, and let stand, undisturbed, at room temperature 24 hours. To check seals, remove the bands, and press down on the center of each lid. If the lid doesn't move, the jar is sealed. If the lid depresses and pops up again, the jar is not sealed. Store properly sealed jars in a cool, dark place up to 1 year. Refrigerate after opening.

little jars, big flavors

Eat these spicy-tart pickles straight up, or pulse them in a food processor to make a quick salsa. If you prefer milder pickles, gently tap the cut peppers to shake out some of the seeds before adding the peppers to the jars.

GREEN TOMATO-HOT PEPPER PICKLES

2½ lb. green tomatoes (about 7 medium), cut into eighths

1 lb. yellow, green, and orange hot banana peppers (Hungarian wax), cut into ½-inch rings

1 lb. Anaheim peppers, cut into ½-inch rings

1 small onion, sliced (1¼ cups)

4 tsp. canning-and-pickling salt, divided

4 cups white vinegar (5% acidity)

½ cup sugar

1 Tbsp. pickling spice

1 Tbsp. mustard seeds

6 small garlic cloves

makes: 6 (1-pt.) widemouthed jars for the shelf

hands-on time: 40 min.

total time: 1 hour, 35 min., plus 3 weeks standing time

1. Sterilize jars, and prepare lids as described on page 22.

2. While jars are boiling, toss together first 4 ingredients and 3 tsp. salt in a very large bowl. Let stand 20 minutes. Drain.

3. Bring vinegar, sugar, remaining 1 tsp. salt, and 2 cups water to a boil in a 12-qt. stainless steel or enameled stockpot, stirring until sugar dissolves.

4. Place ½ tsp. pickling spice, ½ tsp. mustard seeds, and 1 garlic clove in each hot jar. Using a slotted spoon, transfer vegetables to hot jars, packing tightly and leaving ½-inch headspace. Cover vegetables with hot pickling liquid, leaving ½-inch headspace. Seal and process jars as described on pages 22–25, processing 15 minutes.

5. Remove jars from water, and let stand, undisturbed, at room temperature 24 hours. To check seals, remove the bands, and press down on the center of each lid. If the lid doesn't move, the jar is sealed. If the lid depresses and pops up again, the jar is not sealed. Store properly sealed jars in a cool, dark place up to 1 year. Refrigerate after opening.

little jars, big flavors

Add this sweet-and-spicy cauliflower to a muffuletta sandwich, or use to round out a meat-and-cheese tray.

PICKLED CAULIFLOWER

1	large head cauliflower	½	cup diced red bell pepper
2	tsp. canning-and-pickling salt	1	Tbsp. mustard seeds
2¼	cups white vinegar (5% acidity)	1½	tsp. celery seeds
1	cup sugar	½	tsp. ground turmeric
1	cup thin onion slices	½	tsp. dried crushed red pepper

1. Rinse cauliflower, and cut into 1- to 2-inch florets to measure 6 cups. Bring 2 qt. water and salt to a boil in a 6-qt. saucepan. Add cauliflower; blanch 3 minutes. Drain and cool.

2. Sterilize jars, and prepare lids as described on page 22.

3. While jars are boiling, combine vinegar and next 7 ingredients in a large stainless steel saucepan. Bring to a boil; reduce heat, and simmer, uncovered, 5 minutes. Stir drained cauliflower into vinegar-vegetable mixture to distribute. Using a slotted spoon, transfer hot vegetables to hot jars, leaving ½-inch headspace. Cover vegetables with hot pickling liquid, leaving ½-inch headspace.

4. Seal and process jars as described on pages 22–25, processing 10 minutes.

5. Remove jars from water, and let stand, undisturbed, at room temperature 24 hours. To check seals, remove the bands, and press down on the center of each lid. If the lid doesn't move, the jar is sealed. If the lid depresses and pops up again, the jar is not sealed. Store properly sealed jars in a cool, dark place up to 1 year. Refrigerate after opening.

To get thin slices rather than rings for these pickles, cut onions in half vertically, slicing through the root. Then, peel, trim and thinly slice each half radially, cutting from top end to root end. For serious satisfaction, tuck some of the finished pickles into your favorite grilled cheese sandwich.

PICKLED RED ONIONS

2	cups white vinegar (5% acidity)
¾	cup sugar
2	Tbsp. canning-and-pickling salt
8	cups thin slices red onion (about 3 lb.)
1¾	tsp. whole allspice
1¾	tsp. mustard seeds
7	small bay leaves
7	(3-inch) thyme sprigs
7	small dried red chiles (such as bird's beak peppers or pequin chiles)

1. Sterilize jars, and prepare lids as described on page 22.

2. While jars are boiling, combine first 3 ingredients and 1½ cups water in a large stainless steel or enameled Dutch oven; bring to a boil, stirring to dissolve sugar and salt. Add sliced onion to vinegar mixture; reduce heat, and simmer 6 minutes, uncovered, or until onion just begins to soften.

3. Place ¼ tsp. allspice, ¼ tsp. mustard seeds, 1 bay leaf, 1 thyme sprig, and 1 chile pepper in each hot jar. Using tongs, transfer onion to hot jars, leaving ½-inch headspace. Cover onion with hot pickling liquid, leaving ½-inch headspace. Seal and process jars as described on pages 22–25, processing 10 minutes.

4. Remove jars from water, and let stand, undisturbed, at room temperature 24 hours. To check seals, remove the bands, and press down on the center of each lid. If the lid doesn't move, the jar is sealed. If the lid depresses and pops up again, the jar is not sealed. Store properly sealed jars in a cool, dark place up to 1 year. Refrigerate after opening.

makes: 7 (½-pt.) jars for the shelf

hands-on time: 30 min.

total time: 1 hour, plus 3 weeks standing time

little jars, big flavors

At farmers' markets and specialty grocers these days, carrots come in a rainbow of shades. In pickling them all, we discovered a fun fact: Putting even one purple carrot in a jar lends some extra red color to the other carrots, making them more vibrantly orange and orange-red.

PICKLED RAINBOW CARROTS WITH CORIANDER

3½	lb. small (3- to 5-inch) purple, orange, yellow, and white carrots with tops	¼	cup canning-and-pickling salt
		2	tsp. coriander seeds
3½	cups white vinegar (5% acidity)	3 to 4	garlic cloves
		8	dill sprigs

1. Sterilize jars, and prepare lids as described on page 22.

2. While jars are boiling, wash and peel carrots; trim green tops to ¼ inch, and trim any carrots that are longer than 4 inches (so that they'll fit comfortably within the jars). Cut carrots in half lengthwise.

3. Combine vinegar, salt, and 1 cup water in a 4-qt. stainless steel saucepan. Bring to a boil over medium heat, stirring until salt dissolves; reduce heat, and simmer until ready to fill jars.

4. Place ½ tsp. coriander seeds, 1 garlic clove, and 2 dill sprigs in each hot jar. Pack jars tightly with carrots. Cover carrots with hot pickling liquid, leaving ½-inch headspace. Seal and process jars as described on pages 22–25, processing 15 minutes.

5. Remove jars from water and let stand, undisturbed, at room temperature 24 hours. To check seals, remove the bands, and press down on the center of each lid. If the lid doesn't move, the jar is sealed. If the lid depresses and pops up again, the jar is not sealed. Store properly sealed jars in a cool, dark place 3 weeks before tasting. Store jars in a cool, dark place up to 1 year. Refrigerate after opening.

makes: 3 to 4 (1-pt.) widemouthed jars for the shelf

hands-on time: 1 hour, 5 min.

total time: 1 hour, 20 min., plus 3 weeks standing time

Warm spices and a sweet-tart brine make these cherries ideal with duck or pork. Chop a few and add to a cream-cheese-topped biscuit with country ham for a sweet and salty Southern canapé.

PICKLED CHERRIES

2½ cups white vinegar (5% acidity)
2 cups sugar
2 Tbsp. canning-and-pickling salt
1 vanilla bean, split
7 whole cloves
7 star anise
7 (3-inch) cinnamon sticks
2½ lb. fresh dark sweet cherries, washed, stemmed, and pitted

1. Sterilize jars, and prepare lids as described on page 22.

2. While jars are boiling, stir together first 3 ingredients in a medium stainless steel saucepan. Scrape seeds from vanilla bean; add seeds and bean to vinegar mixture. Bring to a boil, stirring until sugar and salt dissolve.

3. Place 1 clove, 1 star anise, and 1 cinnamon stick in each hot jar. Pack cherries tightly into jars, leaving ½-inch headspace (about 12 cherries in each jar). Remove vanilla bean from pan; discard. Cover cherries with hot pickling liquid, leaving ½-inch headspace. Seal and process jars as described on pages 22–25, processing 10 minutes.

4. Remove jars from water, and let stand, undisturbed, at room temperature 24 hours. To check seals, remove the bands, and press down on the center of each lid. If the lid doesn't move, the jar is sealed. If the lid depresses and pops up again, the jar is not sealed. Store properly sealed jars in a cool, dark place up to 1 year. Refrigerate after opening.

makes: 7 (½-pt.) jars for the shelf

hands-on time: 37 min.

total time: 1 hour, 7 min., plus 3 weeks standing time

NOTE: Use a cherry pitter or a large paper clip to pit cherries while leaving them whole.

little jars, big flavors

Use your melon like a Southerner: Eat the flesh, and pickle the rind. Pack these pickles into pint jars and give one to a friend, or tuck them all into a single quart for yourself.

REFRIGERATOR PICKLED WATERMELON RIND

½ small red watermelon (about 5 lb.)	¾ cup sugar
	¾ cup white vinegar (5% acidity)
3 Tbsp. salt	2 star anise

makes: 2 (1-pt.) jars or 1 (1-qt.) jar for the fridge

hands-on time: 30 min.

total time: 1 hour, 35 min., plus 2 days chilling time

1. Place watermelon cut side down on a work surface; slice into ¾-inch slices. Trim all but ¼ inch red flesh from slices. Reserve flesh for another use. Remove outer green layer of rind using a vegetable peeler; discard. Cut rind slices crosswiseinto 1-inch lengths. (You should have about 5 cups.) Place in a large bowl.

2. Stir together salt and 3 cups water; pour over rind. Cover and chill 24 hours. Drain; rinse well.

3. Combine rind, sugar, vinegar, and ¾ cup water in a 4-qt. stainless steel saucepan. Bring to a boil, stirring until sugar dissolves. Remove from heat. Cool completely (about 1 hour), stirring occasionally.

4. Place star anise in clean jars. Using a slotted spoon, transfer rind to jars; cover with pickling liquid. Apply lids. Chill 24 hours before serving. Store in refrigerator up to 1 week.

Habanero pepper makes this salsa extra spicy. Peaches and sugar cut the heat (a little). Try it with tortilla chips or our terrific duck tacos (recipe on next page).

FIERY PEACH SALSA

(recipe on next page)

makes: 7 (½-pt.) jars
for the shelf

hands-on time: 42 min.

total time: 1 hour, 2 min.

6	cups peeled, diced hard, underripe peaches	¼	tsp. salt
1	cup sugar	2	jalapeño peppers, seeded and chopped (2 Tbsp.)
1	cup chopped red bell pepper	2	garlic cloves, minced (1 Tbsp.)
1	cup cider vinegar (5% acidity)	1	habanero pepper, seeded and minced (1 Tbsp.)
½	cup chopped red onion	¼	cup chopped fresh cilantro
¼	cup bottled lime juice		

1. Sterilize jars, and prepare lids as described on page 22.

2. While jars are boiling, combine all ingredients, except cilantro, in an 8-qt. stainless steel or enameled Dutch oven. Add ½ cup water; bring to a boil over high heat, stirring until sugar dissolves. Reduce heat, and simmer 5 minutes. Remove from heat; stir in cilantro.

3. Fill, seal, and process jars as described on pages 22–25, leaving ½-inch headspace and processing 10 minutes.

4. Remove jars from water, and let stand, undisturbed, at room temperature 24 hours. To check seals, remove the bands, and press down on the center of each lid. If the lid doesn't move, the jar is sealed. If the lid depresses and pops up again, the jar is not sealed. Store properly sealed jars in a cool, dark place up to 1 year. Refrigerate after opening.

little jars, big flavors

SEARED DUCK TACOS WITH FIERY PEACH SALSA

4   boned duck breasts (1½ lb.)
¾   tsp. garlic salt
¼   tsp. freshly ground pepper
8   (6-inch) corn-flour blend tortillas
1   cup loosely packed arugula
1   cup Fiery Peach Salsa (previous page)
2   oz. crumbled goat cheese

1. Sprinkle duck with salt and pepper. Heat a large skillet over medium-high heat. Add duck, skin side down, to skillet. Cook 6 minutes on each side or to desired degree of doneness. Remove duck from pan. Let stand 5 minutes.

2. Meanwhile, wrap tortillas in a damp paper towel. Microwave at HIGH 30 seconds or until warm. Remove skin from duck, and cut diagonally across the grain into thin slices. Fill tortillas evenly with duck slices, arugula, salsa, and cheese; fold in half.

NOTE: We tested with Don Pancho half-flour, half-corn tortillas.

makes: 4 servings for the table

hands-on time: 23 min.

total time: 23 min.

little jars, big flavors

This smoky relish is delicious with grilled salmon, chicken, and flank steak. It also makes a wonderful addition to burritos and omelets.

GRILLED VEGETABLE RELISH

3	garlic bulbs
3	Tbsp. olive oil, divided
3	large dried chipotle peppers
4½	lb. plum tomatoes (16 large), halved lengthwise and seeded
8	oz. shallots (4 large), peeled and cut in half lengthwise
2	lb. onions (about 3 medium), peeled and cut into ½-inch-thick slices
¾	cup chopped fresh cilantro
¾	cup fresh lime juice (about 4 limes)
1½	tsp. salt

1. Preheat oven to 425°. Cut off pointed end of each garlic bulb. Place each bulb on a 6-inch piece of aluminum foil, drizzle with 1 tsp. oil, and wrap with foil. Bake at 425° for 30 minutes; let cool 10 minutes. Squeeze pulp from garlic bulbs into a food processor.

2. While garlic bakes, remove stem and seeds from chipotle peppers; place in a small bowl, and cover with boiling water. Let stand 30 minutes; drain, discarding liquid. Coarsely chop peppers.

3. Preheat grill to medium-high heat. Place tomato halves and shallots in a large bowl. Drizzle with 1 Tbsp. oil, and toss gently to coat. Brush onion slices with remaining 1 Tbsp. oil. Working in 2 batches, place onion slices, shallot halves, and tomato halves skin side

down on grill. Grill 10 minutes or until tomato skins are blistered and beginning to char and onion and shallots are tender, turning halfway through. Transfer to a large bowl. Let cool 10 minutes.

4. Remove skins from tomatoes. Chop onion slices and shallots into large pieces; place in a large bowl, and toss well. Add chipotle peppers, and one-third of tomato-and-onion mixture (including any accumulated juices) to roasted garlic in food processor; pulse 5 times or until chopped, then pour into a 4-qt. stainless steel saucepan. Repeat procedure twice with remaining tomato and onion mixture.

5. Sterilize jars, and prepare lids as described on page 22. While jars are boiling, bring tomato mixture to a boil over medium heat, stirring occasionally; remove from heat. Stir in cilantro and next 2 ingredients.

6. Fill, seal, and process jars as described on pages 22–25, leaving ½-inch headspace and processing 15 minutes.

7. Remove jars from water, and let stand, undisturbed, at room temperature 24 hours. To check seals, remove the bands, and press down on the center of each lid. If the lid doesn't move, the jar is sealed. If the lid depresses and pops up again, the jar is not sealed. Store properly sealed jars in a cool, dark place up to 1 year. Refrigerate after opening.

makes: 3 (1-pt.) jars for the shelf

hands-on time: 1 hour, 41 min.

total time: 2 hours, 21 min., plus 1 day standing time

Tangy, spicy, and sweet, here's a chutney to pair with goat cheese, bacon, and chicken.

HEIRLOOM TOMATO CHUTNEY

4¾ lb. red heirloom tomatoes	¾ tsp. dried crushed red pepper
1 large onion, cut into eighths	¾ tsp. ground allspice
1 cup sugar	½ tsp. salt
⅔ cup white vinegar (5% acidity)	

makes: 4 (½-pt.) widemouthed jars for the shelf

hands-on time: 1 hour, 54 min.

total time: 2 hours, 4 min.

1. Cut a large "X" in bottom of each tomato. Working in batches, place tomatoes in a wire basket, and lower into a large pot of boiling water. Blanch 30 to 60 seconds or until skins start to split. Dip immediately into ice water; drain. Working over a bowl to collect juices, remove skins, and cut out cores; quarter tomatoes, and add to bowl.

2. Sterilize jars, and prepare lids as described on page 22.

3. While jars are boiling, pulse onion in a food processor in batches until chopped to measure 2 cups. Place onion in a 4-qt. stainless steel saucepan.

4. Process tomato quarters and any accumulated juices in food processor in 2 batches just until chopped. Add chopped tomato and juices to onion. Add sugar and remaining ingredients. Bring to a boil over medium-high heat. Cook, uncovered, 1 hour and 5 minutes or until mixture is thick and reduced to 4 cups, stirring often.

5. Fill, seal, and process jars as described on pages 22–25, leaving ¼-inch headspace and processing 10 minutes.

6. Remove jars from water, and let stand, undisturbed, at room temperature 24 hours. To check seals, remove the bands, and press down on the center of each lid. If the lid doesn't move, the jar is sealed. If the lid depresses and pops up again, the jar is not sealed. Store properly sealed jars in a cool, dark place up to 1 year. Refrigerate after opening.

little jars, big flavors

GREEN TOMATO CHOWCHOW

6   cups coarsely chopped green tomatoes (2 lb.)

2   cups chopped Vidalia onion (1 large)

½   cup diced red bell pepper

⅓   cup seeded and minced red jalapeño pepper

1   Tbsp. kosher salt

1   cup cider vinegar (5% acidity)

⅔   cup sugar

1   tsp. dried crushed red pepper

2   tsp. sorghum syrup

½   tsp. celery seeds

1. Working in batches, pulse tomatoes and onion in a food processor 15 times or just until finely chopped. Transfer to a 6-qt. stainless steel or enameled Dutch oven. Stir in peppers and salt. Cover and chill 8 to 24 hours.

2. Uncover and bring to a rolling boil over medium-high heat, stirring occasionally. Pour through a wire-mesh strainer into a bowl, pressing with back of a spoon to release liquid. Discard liquid; return solids to Dutch oven.

3. Add remaining ingredients; bring to a boil over medium-high heat. Boil, stirring occasionally, 3 minutes or until liquid evaporates. Spoon into clean jars or other heatproof, nonreactive containers with lids. Let cool slightly. Cover and chill; store in refrigerator up to 3 weeks.

makes: 4 (½-pt.) jars for the fridge

hands-on time: 35 min.

total time: 45 min.,
plus 1 day for chilling

little jars, big flavors

BEER-BATTERED GROUPER WITH GREEN TOMATO CHOWCHOW

Vegetable oil
6   (6-oz.) grouper fillets
¾   tsp. salt
½   tsp. freshly ground black pepper
1½   cups all-purpose flour
¼   cup self-rising white cornmeal mix
⅓   tsp. ground red pepper
1   (12-oz.) bottle lager beer
1½   cups Green Tomato Chowchow (previous page)

1. Pour oil to depth of 3 inches into a large Dutch oven; heat to 375°. Sprinkle fish evenly with salt and black pepper.

2. Combine flour, cornmeal mix, and red pepper in a large bowl. Whisk in beer. Dip fish in batter, allowing excess to drip off.

3. Fry fish, in 2 batches, 6 minutes or until golden brown (do not turn). Drain fish on a wire rack over paper towels. Serve fish with Green Tomato Chowchow.

makes: 6 servings for the table

hands-on time: 24 min.

total time: 24 min.

The hint of cinnamon makes these tomatoes ideal for pastitsio, moussaka, eggplant Parmesan, and chili.

MEDITERRANEAN-STYLE TOMATOES

6	lb. firm ripe red heirloom tomatoes	8	garlic cloves, pressed
1	Tbsp. salt	2	Tbsp. minced fresh oregano
2	(3-inch) cinnamon sticks	¼	cup bottled lemon juice

makes: 4 (1-pt.) jars for the shelf

hands-on time: 1 hour, 33 min.

total time: 2 hours, 36 min., plus 1 week standing time

1. Cut a large "X" in bottom of each tomato. Working in batches, place tomatoes in a wire basket, and lower into a large pot of boiling water. Blanch 30 to 60 seconds or until skins start to split. Dip immediately into ice water; drain. Working over an 8-qt. stainless steel or enameled Dutch oven to collect juices, remove skins, and cut out cores; cut tomatoes into 1½-inch chunks, and add to Dutch oven. Stir in salt, cinnamon sticks, and garlic. Cover and bring to a boil over medium-high heat. Uncover and boil 5 minutes, stirring occasionally. Remove from heat; let stand, covered, 30 minutes.

2. Sterilize jars, and prepare lids as described on page 22.

3. Stir oregano into tomato mixture; return to a boil. Remove and discard cinnamon sticks. Stir lemon juice into tomato mixture.

4. Fill, seal, and process jars as described on pages 22–25, leaving ½-inch headspace and processing 35 minutes.

5. Remove jars from water, and let stand, undisturbed, at room temperature 24 hours. To check seals, remove the bands, and press down on the center of each lid. If the lid doesn't move, the jar is sealed. If the lid depresses and pops up again, the jar is not sealed. Store properly sealed jars in a cool, dark place up to 1 year. Refrigerate after opening.

One good tomato haul yields a few potent jars of this tasty sauce. If you have an abundance of tomatoes and four burners, you can prepare up to three batches, each in its own Dutch oven, concurrently, and process the jars for all three batches in the same canning pot. If you have more freezer space than time to can, you can freeze this delicious sauce in zip-top plastic freezer bags.

CHUNKY MARINARA SAUCE WITH RED WINE

10   lb. firm, ripe tomatoes
1½   cups chopped onions
¾   cup shredded carrot (about 2 medium)
⅓   cup finely chopped fresh basil
3   Tbsp. finely chopped fresh oregano
5   garlic cloves, minced
1   cup dry red wine
3   Tbsp. bottled lemon juice
2   Tbsp. olive oil
2¼   tsp. salt
1   tsp. sugar
½   tsp. freshly ground pepper

1. Cut a large "X" in bottom of each tomato. Working in batches, place tomatoes in a wire basket, and lower into a large pot of boiling water. Blanch 30 to 60 seconds or until skins start to split. Dip immediately into ice water; drain. Working over an 8-qt. stainless steel or enameled Dutch oven to collect juices, remove skins, and cut out cores; halve tomatoes, and add to Dutch oven. Reserving seeds in Dutch oven, seed and chop enough of the tomatoes to equal 3 cups of ½-inch dice. Set aside diced tomatoes

in a large bowl. Add onion and next 4 ingredients to Dutch oven. Cover and bring to a boil, stirring occasionally. Reduce heat, and simmer 1 hour. Remove from heat and cool 10 minutes.

2. Puree cooked mixture in batches in food processor until smooth. Pour through a fine wire-mesh strainer into the bowl with the diced tomatoes, pressing mixture with a wooden spoon to release juices. Discard seeds and any remaining pulp. Pour tomato mixture into Dutch oven; add wine and next 5 ingredients. Partially cover and cook over low heat about 2 hours or until mixture reduces to 6 cups, stirring occasionally to keep from scorching.

3. During the last 20 minutes of cooking, sterilize jars, and prepare lids as described on page 22.

4. Fill, seal, and process jars as described on pages 22–25, leaving ¼-inch headspace and processing 45 minutes.

5. Remove jars from water and let stand, undisturbed, at room temperature 24 hours. To check seals, remove the bands, and press down on the center of each lid. If the lid doesn't move, the jar is sealed. If the lid depresses and pops up again, the jar is not sealed. Store properly sealed jars in a cool, dark place up to 1 year. Refrigerate after opening.

makes: 3 (1-pt.) jars for the shelf

hands-on time: 1 hour, 50 min.

total time: 6 hours,
plus 1 day standing time

little jars, big flavors

EASY FREEZER
PRESERVES

6

If you're new to canning, freezer preserves are an excellent place to start. Most use instant pectin, need minimal cooking, and are not processed in boiling water. Even if you're an old hand at putting up, you'll appreciate this recipe. It's as easy and sunny as a Southern Saturday morning, and it won't heat up your kitchen.

ORANGE-PINEAPPLE FREEZER PRESERVES

1½ cups sugar
2½ cups chopped orange sections (6 medium)
2 Tbsp. lemon juice
1 (8-oz.) can crushed pineapple in juice, undrained
2 (0.6-oz.) packages instant pectin

makes: 4 (½-pt.) jars for the freezer

hands-on time: 10 min.

total time: 55 min.

1. Stir together first 4 ingredients in a medium glass or nonmetallic bowl. Let stand 15 minutes.

2. Gradually stir in pectin; stir 3 minutes. Let stand 30 minutes.

3. Spoon mixture into clean (½-pt.) jars or other freezer containers, leaving ½-inch headspace. Seal, label, and freeze upright. Store in freezer up to 1 year. Thaw completely (about 1 day) in refrigerator before using. Refrigerate after thawing, and use within 3 weeks.

NOTE: We tested with Ball RealFruit Instant Pectin.

Because it's uncooked, this simple berry jam tastes incredibly fresh. Even if you pull it out of the freezer in January, you'll think you're eating just-picked berries.

STRAWBERRY-BLUEBERRY FREEZER JAM

makes: 5 (½-pt.) jars for the freezer

hands-on time: 20 min.

total time: 40 min.

4 **cups fresh blueberries (1 lb., 5 oz.)**

3 **cups halved fresh strawberries (12 oz.)**

1½ **cups sugar**

1 **(1.59-oz.) package freezer jam pectin**

1. Pulse blueberries in a food processor 18 times or until finely chopped, stopping to scrape down sides as needed. Place in a medium bowl. Pulse strawberries in food processor 15 times or until finely chopped, stopping to scrape down sides as needed. Add to blueberries in bowl. Stir in sugar; let stand 15 minutes.

2. Gradually stir in pectin; stir 3 minutes. Let stand 5 minutes.

3. Spoon mixture into clean (½-pt.) jars or other freezer containers, leaving ½-inch headspace. Seal, label, and freeze upright. Store in freezer up to 1 year. Thaw completely (about 1 day) in refrigerator before using. Refrigerate after thawing, and use within 3 weeks.

NOTE: We tested with Ball Fruit Jell Freezer Jam Pectin.

BLUEBERRY-RASPBERRY FREEZER JAM

3   cups fresh blueberries (1 lb.)
2¾ cups fresh raspberries (12 oz.)
1¾ cups sugar
1   Tbsp. lemon zest
2   Tbsp. fresh lemon juice
1   (1.59-oz.) package freezer jam pectin

1. Pulse blueberries in a food processor 3 times or until crushed to measure 2 cups, stopping to scrape down sides.

2. Place raspberries in a large glass or nonmetallic bowl; mash with a potato masher until crushed. Add blueberries, sugar, and next 2 ingredients, stirring well. Let stand 15 minutes.

3. Gradually stir in pectin; stir 3 minutes. Let stand 30 minutes.

4. Spoon mixture into clean (½-pt.) jars or other freezer containers, leaving ½-inch headspace. Seal, label, and freeze upright. Store in freezer up to 1 year. Thaw completely (about 1 day) in refrigerator before using. Refrigerate after thawing, and use within 3 weeks.

NOTE: We tested with Ball Fruit Jell Freezer Jam Pectin.

makes: 5 (½-pt.) jars for the freezer

hands-on time: 10 min.

total time: 55 min.

For an even sweeter start to the morning, substitute glazed walnuts or candied pecans for the toasted walnut topping.

BLUEBERRY-RASPBERRY STEEL-CUT OATS

½   cup chopped walnuts

4   cups milk

2   Tbsp. light brown sugar

¼   tsp. ground cinnamon

¼   tsp. salt

1   cup steel-cut oats

½   cup Blueberry-Raspberry Freezer Jam (previous page)

1. Preheat oven to 350°. Bake walnuts in a single layer in a shallow pan 5 minutes or until toasted and fragrant, stirring halfway through.

2. Combine milk and next 3 ingredients in a large saucepan. Cook over medium heat, stirring often, 3 to 4 minutes or just until bubbles appear (do not boil).

3. Stir in oats. Cook, uncovered, over low heat, stirring often, 30 to 35 minutes or until thick and creamy. Remove from heat; stir in jam. Spoon into bowls; sprinkle with walnuts.

makes: 4 servings for the table

hands-on time: 45 min.

total time: 45 min.

little jars, big flavors

Use this chunky, sweet-tart jam as a spread on a grilled Cheddar panini or as a topping for sweet potato biscuits with prosciutto or country ham.

GRANNY SMITH APPLE FREEZER JAM

5 cups coarsely chopped, unpeeled Granny Smith apples (1¾ lb.)

1 cup sugar

½ cup pasteurized apple juice

1 tsp. lemon juice

1 (1.59-oz.) package freezer jam pectin

makes: 4 (½-pt.) jars for the freezer

hands-on time: 20 min.

total time: 40 min.

1. Pulse half of chopped apples in a food processor 21 times or until finely chopped, stopping to scrape down sides as needed. Place in a medium glass or nonmetallic bowl. Repeat procedure with remaining half of apples. Stir in sugar and juices; let stand 15 minutes.

2. Gradually stir in pectin; stir 3 minutes. Let stand 5 minutes.

3. Spoon mixture into clean (½-pt.) jars or other freezer containers, leaving ½-inch headspace. Seal, label, and freeze upright. Store in freezer up to 1 year. Thaw completely (about 1 day) in refrigerator before using. Refrigerate after thawing, and use within 3 weeks.

NOTE: We tested with Ball Fruit Jell Freezer Jam Pectin.

little jars, big flavors

These rosy-peach colored preserves have brilliant fruit flavor and pretty flecks of bright red plum skin. We found they gelled best with standard powdered pectin rather than the instant or freezer pectin that we usually prefer for freezer jam.

PEACH-PLUM FREEZER JAM

1   lb. red plums (about 5 plums), pitted and quartered
1½ cups diced peeled fresh peaches (¾ lb., 2 large)
3   cups sugar
2   Tbsp. lemon juice
1   (1¾-oz.) package powdered pectin

1. Pulse plum quarters in a food processor until minced. Measure 2 cups minced plums, and place in a large glass or nonmetallic bowl. Stir in peaches, sugar, and lemon juice.

2. Combine ¾ cup water and pectin in a small stainless steel saucepan. Bring to a boil. Boil 1 minute. Add pectin mixture to fruit mixture, stirring gently for 3 minutes. Let cool completely (about 1 hour).

3. Spoon mixture into clean (½-pt.) jars or other freezer containers, leaving ½-inch headspace. Seal, label, and freeze upright. Store in freezer up to 1 year. Thaw completely (about 1 day) in refrigerator before using. Refrigerate after thawing, and use within 3 weeks.

NOTE: We tested with Sure-Jell Premium Fruit Pectin.

STRAWBERRY-RHUBARB FREEZER JAM

2   cups sugar, divided
3   cups frozen strawberries, partially thawed
3   cups frozen sliced rhubarb, partially thawed
1   (1.59-oz.) package freezer jam pectin

1. Stir 1 cup sugar into the strawberries, and let stand at room temperature. Cook rhubarb with remaining 1 cup sugar in a medium stainless steel saucepan over medium heat 10 minutes or until fruit is softened and sugar is melted, stirring constantly.

2. Stir strawberry mixture into rhubarb mixture; pulse in a food processor 8 to 12 times or until slightly chunky, stopping to scrape down sides. Transfer to a medium glass or nonmetallic bowl. Let stand 15 minutes. Gradually stir in pectin. Stir 3 minutes; let stand 30 minutes.

3. Spoon mixture into clean (½-pt.) jars or other freezer containers, leaving ½-inch headspace. Seal, label, and freeze upright. Store in freezer up to 1 year. Thaw completely (about 1 day) in refrigerator before using. Refrigerate after thawing, and use within 3 weeks.

NOTE: We tested with Ball Fruit Jell Freezer Jam Pectin.

makes: 4 (½-pt.) jars
for the freezer

———

hands-on time: 15 min.

———

total time: 1 hour

little jars, big flavors

This smoothie works with any of our freezer jams, but we like the strawberry, rhubarb, and banana combination.

STRAWBERRY-RHUBARB-BANANA SMOOTHIE

1	cup plain low-fat yogurt
¼	cup Strawberry-Rhubarb Freezer Jam, thawed (previous page)
2½	cups frozen unsweetened strawberries
¼	tsp. lemon zest
1	Tbsp. fresh lemon juice
2	bananas, peeled and broken into pieces

1. Place yogurt and jam in a blender. Add strawberries and remaining ingredients; process until smooth.

makes: 4 cups for the table

hands-on time: 6 min.

total time: 6 min.

little jars, big flavors

These sweet pickles will win over even those who prefer sour pickles. For the best results and easiest packing, slice a small sweet onion or use only the small inner rings from a larger onion.

LIME-MINT FREEZER PICKLES

2½ lb. (3- to 5-inch) pickling cucumbers, thinly sliced

¼ cup canning-and-pickling salt

1½ cups sugar

1 cup white vinegar (5% acidity)

1 cup chopped red bell pepper

½ cup thinly sliced sweet onion (small rings)

¼ cup finely chopped fresh mint

1 Tbsp. lime zest (2 medium)

2 garlic cloves, minced

1. Toss together sliced cucumbers and salt in a large glass or nonmetallic bowl. Cover and let stand 3 hours; drain, and return to bowl.

2. Add sugar and next 6 ingredients; stir well. Cover and chill 8 hours.

3. Drain cucumber mixture, reserving liquid. Pack cucumbers into clean (½-pt.) canning jars or other freezer containers, leaving 1-inch headspace. Pour reserved liquid over cucumber mixture, leaving ½-inch headspace. Seal, label, and freeze upright. Store in freezer up to 6 months. Thaw completely (about 1 day) in refrigerator before using. Refrigerate after thawing, and use within 1 week.

makes: 5 to 6 (½-pt.) jars for the freezer

hands-on time: 55 min.

total time: 55 minutes, plus 8 hours chilling time

little jars, big flavors

The unique tzatziki sauce uses freezer pickles instead of fresh cucumbers.

LAMB KABOBS WITH TZATZIKI SAUCE

makes: 4 servings
for the table

hands-on time: 32 min.

total time: 1 hour, 2 min.

5	Tbsp. fresh lemon juice, divided
2	Tbsp. olive oil
2	tsp. Dijon mustard
2	Tbsp. chopped fresh mint
1	tsp. salt
1	tsp. freshly ground pepper
2	garlic cloves, minced
1	(1½-lb.) boneless leg of lamb, cut into 1½-inch pieces
2	small red onions, cut into 1-inch wedges
1	red bell pepper, cut into 8 (1½-inch) wedges
4	(14-inch) metal skewers
⅔	cup plain low-fat yogurt
⅓	cup Lime-Mint Freezer Pickles (page 209), drained and chopped

Pita bread

Garnishes: lemon wedges, chopped fresh mint

1. Combine ¼ cup lemon juice and next 6 ingredients in a large zip-top plastic freezer bag. Add lamb to bag; seal bag, turning to coat. Chill 30 minutes.

2. Meanwhile, preheat grill to 350° to 400° (medium-high) heat. Remove lamb from marinade, discarding marinade, and pat dry with paper towels. Thread lamb and vegetables alternately onto skewers. Grill 5 minutes on each side or until desired degree of doneness.

3. Combine yogurt, pickles, and remaining 1 Tbsp. lemon juice in a small bowl. Serve with lamb kabobs and pita bread. Garnish with lemon wedges and chopped mint.

This easy pickle starts in the microwave, moves to the fridge, and finishes in the freezer, so there's no heating up your kitchen. Look for pickling cucumbers—the small, crisp, unwaxed sort—at farmers' markets and grocery stores. Because their skins are neither tough nor bitter, they don't have to be peeled.

PEPPERY TEXAS FREEZER PICKLES

2 lb. (3- to 5-inch) pickling cucumbers, sliced ¼ inch thick

1 large sweet onion, halved and thinly sliced

1 cup fresh cilantro

6 small dried red chile peppers

4 garlic cloves, thinly sliced

3 cups white vinegar (5% acidity)

⅓ cup sugar

2 Tbsp. canning-and-pickling salt

1 Tbsp. pickling spice

1. Place first 5 ingredients in a large glass or nonmetallic bowl.

2. Combine vinegar, next 3 ingredients, and 1 cup water in a 2-qt. glass measuring cup. Microwave at HIGH 3 minutes or until hot, stirring until sugar dissolves. Pour hot mixture evenly over cucumber mixture, stirring well. Cover and chill 48 hours.

3. Drain cucumber mixture, reserving liquid. Pack cucumbers into clean (1-pt.) canning jars or other freezer containers, leaving 1½-inch headspace. Pour liquid over cucumber mixture, leaving 1-inch headspace. Seal, label, and freeze upright. Store in freezer up to 6 months. Thaw completely (about 1 day) in refrigerator before using. Refrigerate after thawing, and use within 1 week.

makes: 5 to 6 (½-pt.) jars for the freezer

hands-on time: 55 min.

total time: 55 minutes, plus 8 hours chilling time

Not only will this chunky relish take hot dogs to a new level, it's also tasty spooned over grilled chicken, fish, and pork.

HOT-AND-SWEET FREEZER PICKLE RELISH

makes: 4 (½-pt.) jars
for the freezer

hands-on time: 30 min.

total time: 30 min.,
plus 2 days chilling time

3½ cups diced (3- to 5-inch) pickling cucumbers (1 lb.)
1⅓ cups chopped onion (1 medium)
1   cup finely chopped red bell pepper (1 medium)
2   jalapeño peppers, seeded and minced
3   large garlic cloves, minced
1   Tbsp. salt
1   cup sugar
1   cup white vinegar (5% acidity)

1. Stir together first 6 ingredients in a large glass or nonmetallic bowl.

2. Combine sugar, vinegar, and 2 Tbsp. water in a medium stainless steel saucepan; cook over medium heat 3 minutes or until sugar dissolves, stirring often. Remove from heat; let stand 5 minutes. Pour vinegar mixture over cucumber mixture. Cover and chill 48 hours.

3. Drain mixture, reserving liquid. Pack mixture into clean (½-pt.) canning jars or other freezer containers, leaving ¾-inch headspace. Pour liquid over cucumber mixture, leaving ½-inch headspace. Seal, label, and freeze upright. Store in freezer up to 6 months. Thaw completely (about 1 day) in refrigerator before using. Refrigerate after thawing, and use within 1 week.

BASIL-PECAN FREEZER PESTO

1   cup pecan pieces
4   oz. Asiago cheese, cut into ½-inch cubes
4   garlic cloves, peeled
3   cups loosely packed fresh basil leaves
1   cup loosely packed fresh flat-leaf parsley
2   Tbsp. fresh rosemary leaves
2   tsp. lemon zest
½   tsp. salt
⅓   tsp. ground red pepper
1   cup olive oil

1. Preheat oven to 350°. Bake pecans in a single layer in a shallow pan 5 minutes or until toasted and fragrant, stirring halfway through. Let cool slightly.

2. Pulse cheese cubes in a large food processor until finely chopped. Add pecans, garlic, and next 6 ingredients. Process until minced. With processor running, pour oil through food chute; process until blended, scraping sides as necessary.

3. Divide mixture evenly among ½-cup jars or other freezer containers. Seal, label, and store upright in freezer up to 6 months. Refrigerate after thawing, and use within 1 week.

makes: 5 (½-cup) jars
for the freezer

hands-on time: 21 min.

total time: 21 min.

CHICKEN PASTA WITH PESTO CREAM SAUCE

½ cup coarsely chopped pecans

8 oz. uncooked linguine

2 tsp. olive oil

1½ lb. skinned and boned chicken breasts, cut into
   1-inch pieces

½ tsp. salt

½ tsp. freshly ground pepper

1 cup half-and-half

¾ cup Basil-Pecan Freezer Pesto (previous page), thawed

1 cup chopped tomato

1. Preheat oven to 350°. Bake pecans in a single layer in a shallow pan 5 minutes or until toasted and fragrant, stirring halfway through.

2. Cook pasta according to package directions. Drain and keep warm. Meanwhile, heat oil in a large skillet over medium-high heat. Sprinkle chicken with salt and pepper. Add chicken to skillet; cook, stirring often, 8 to 10 minutes or until browned and done.

3. Gradually stir half-and-half into pesto in small bowl. Add pesto mixture to chicken; cook 2 minutes or until thickened. Stir in tomato. Add linguine, tossing to coat. Sprinkle with pecans. Serve immediately.

makes: 4 servings for the table

hands-on time: 20 min.

total time: 20 min.

little jars, big flavors

A LITTLE
SOMETHIN'
EXTRA

7

This is something every baker should have. It's more flavorful and usually less expensive than store-bought vanilla, and it makes a wonderful gift. Why heat the alcohol? It helps speed up the infusion. Use whole vanilla beans to make your first bottles. When you're running low on vanilla after that, you can add scraped-out beans (from other recipes that use the seeds) to each bottle, and top off with more alcohol.

BOTTOMLESS VANILLA EXTRACT

3   vanilla beans   3   cups 80-proof vodka or bourbon

1. Cut 1 vanilla bean in half lengthwise. Scrape seeds into a clean (½-pt.) jar. Cut scraped bean pod in half crosswise, and add to jar. Repeat procedure with remaining beans and 2 more clean jars.

2. Place vodka in a medium saucepan. Cook over medium heat 5 minutes or until thoroughly heated. Pour 1 cup vodka over bean pod and vanilla bean seeds in each jar. Let cool to room temperature.

3. Cover jars with tight-fitting lids, and store at room temperature 1 week, shaking daily, before using. If desired, strain liquid into clean decorative bottles with tight-fitting lids, and discard solids. Store in a cool, dark place indefinitely.

NOTE: The vodka-based version has the purest vanilla flavor. Though both extracts turn a rich brown after one week, the bourbon-based version is a smidge darker. Both are delicious in frostings and baked goods.

makes: 3 (½-pt.) jars
for the shelf

———————

hands-on time: 15 min.

———————

total time: 1 hour, 5 min.,
plus 1 week standing time

little jars, big flavors

It takes a lot of berries to make a good syrup, but we love this two-for-one recipe because it gets you a delicious syrup plus all the berry pulp you need for Blueberry Butter (page 68).

BLUEBERRY SYRUP

12 cups fresh blueberries (about 4¼ lb.)
Cheesecloth

3 cups sugar
1½ Tbsp. lemon juice

1. Wash and drain blueberries. Combine blueberries and 2 cups water in an 8-qt. stainless steel or enameled Dutch oven; bring to a boil over medium-high heat, crushing berries with a potato masher. Reduce heat, and simmer 12 minutes, stirring occasionally.

2. Line a fine wire-mesh strainer with 3 layers of dampened cheesecloth. Place strainer over a bowl. Pour blueberry mixture into strainer. (Do not press mixture.) Let stand 30 minutes or until collected juice measures 2½ cups and mixture no longer drips. Reserve pulp (you should have 5½ cups) for Blueberry Butter or another use.

3. Combine 3 cups sugar and 1 cup water in a large stainless steel saucepan. Bring to a boil, stirring until sugar dissolves. Boil 20 minutes or until mixture registers 220° on a candy thermometer, stirring occasionally. Stir in blueberry juice and lemon juice. Return to a boil; reduce heat, and simmer, uncovered, 5 minutes, stirring once. Remove from heat; let foam settle (about 1 minute). Skim off and discard any foam.

4. While mixture reduces, sterilize jars, and prepare lids as described on page 22.

5. Fill, seal, and process jars as described on pages 22–25, leaving ¼-inch headspace and processing 10 minutes.

6. Remove jars from water, and let stand, undisturbed, at room temperature 24 hours. To check seals, remove the bands, and press down on the center of each lid. If the lid doesn't move, the jar is sealed. If the lid depresses and pops up again, the jar is not sealed. Store properly sealed jars in a cool, dark place up to 1 year. Refrigerate after opening.

makes: 4 (½-pt.) jars
for the shelf

hands-on time: 55 min.

total time: 1 hour, 40 min.

little jars, big flavors

Over waffles, cheesecake, or ice cream, this sweet syrup delights.

PEACH-VANILLA SYRUP

6   cups coarsely chopped peeled   ⅛   tsp. salt
    ripe peaches (about 2½ lb.)   Cheesecloth
1½ cups sugar   1   vanilla bean
2   Tbsp. lemon juice

makes: 1 cup
for the fridge

hands-on time: 20 min.

total time: 3 hours, 5 min.

NOTE: For an easy peach butter, process the peach solids in a food processor until smooth. Sweeten with honey to taste. Cover and store in the refrigerator up to 1 week. Use atop biscuits or stir into muffin batters or yogurt.

1. Place peaches in an 8-qt. stainless steel or enameled Dutch oven. Stir in sugar, lemon juice, and salt. Let stand 15 minutes, stirring occasionally. Add 1½ cups water. Bring to a boil; reduce heat to medium, and simmer 10 minutes or until peaches are very soft and lose their shape.

2. Line a fine wire-mesh strainer with 3 layers of dampened cheesecloth. Place strainer over a bowl. Pour peach mixture into strainer. (Do not press mixture.) Let stand 30 minutes or until collected juice measures 3 cups. Discard peach solids or reserve for another use.

3. Transfer juice to a stainless steel saucepan. Cut vanilla bean in half lengthwise, and scrape out seeds with the back of a knife. Add vanilla bean and seeds to peach liquid. Bring to a boil; reduce heat, and simmer, uncovered, stirring occasionally, 45 minutes or until mixture registers 220° on a candy thermometer and syrup coats the back of a metal spoon. Cool completely (1 hour).

4. Skim off and discard any foam. Remove vanilla bean. Pour syrup into a clean (½-pt.) jar, bottle, or other container with a lid. Cover and store in refrigerator up to 3 weeks.

Look for rose water, or rose flower water, in the baking aisle at Middle Eastern, organic, and better grocery stores. It's incredibly fragrant, so a little dab will do. Used sparingly, it adds a soft floral edge to sweet-tart rhubarb. Use the syrup to top cheesecake or ice cream, spike a gin and tonic or a vodka-lemonade, or create a refreshing homemade soda by mixing 3 Tbsp. with 1 cup club soda and plenty of ice.

RHUBARB AND ROSE WATER SYRUP

8   cups (½-inch) cubed rhubarb
2   cups sugar
⅛   tsp. salt

½   cup fresh orange juice
Cheesecloth
½   tsp. rose water

makes: 1¾ cups for the fridge

hands-on time: 20 min.

total time: 2 hours, 15 min., plus 5 days chilling time

1. Stir together first 3 ingredients in an 8-qt. stainless steel or enameled Dutch oven. Let stand 30 minutes, stirring occasionally. Add orange juice and 1½ cups water. Bring to a boil; reduce heat, and simmer, partially covered, 20 minutes or until rhubarb is soft enough to crush with a spoon against side of pan, stirring occasionally.

2. Line a fine wire-mesh strainer with 3 layers of dampened cheesecloth. Place strainer over a bowl. Pour rhubarb mixture into strainer. (Do not press mixture.) Let stand 30 minutes or until collected juice measures 3 cups. Discard rhubarb solids, or reserve for another use.

3. Bring rhubarb liquid to a boil in a clean 6-qt. stainless steel or enameled Dutch oven; reduce heat, and simmer, uncovered, 35 minutes or until mixture registers 220° on a candy thermometer and syrup coats the back of a metal spoon. Remove from heat; cool completely.

4. Stir in rose water. Pour syrup into a clean (1-pt.) jar, bottle, or other container with a lid. Cover and chill 5 days before using for best flavor. Use within 3 weeks.

NOTE: For an easy rhubarb butter, process the rhubarb solids in a food processor until smooth. Sweeten with honey to taste. Cover and store in the refrigerator for up to 1 week. Use atop biscuits or stir into muffin batters or yogurt.

little jars, big flavors

Use this pretty and fragrant vinegar in place of standard vinegar in your favorite vinaigrette.

SPICED BLUEBERRY VINEGAR

2   cups blueberries
1   cup cider vinegar, divided
2   tsp. whole allspice
1   tsp. whole cloves
1   (3- x 1-inch) piece lemon rind
1   (3-inch) cinnamon stick, broken in half
Cheesecloth

1. Wash and drain blueberries. Place berries in a medium glass or nonmetallic bowl. Add ½ cup vinegar; mash blueberries with a potato masher. Stir in remaining vinegar, allspice, and next 3 ingredients. Cover with plastic wrap, and let stand in a cool, dark place 2 days.

2. Line a fine wire-mesh strainer with 3 layers of dampened cheesecloth. Place strainer over a small stainless steel saucepan. Pour blueberry mixture into strainer. Let stand 30 minutes or until dripping stops. Discard solids. Bring vinegar to a boil over medium heat.

3. Pour hot vinegar through a funnel into a clean, dry bottle with a cork or nonmetallic stopper. Let stand until completely cool. Seal and store in refrigerator up to 1 month.

Refreshing herb-infused vinegars add instant flavor to marinades and salad dressings, and they're easy to make and improvise, especially if you grow some herbs of your own. For the best flavor, gather the herbs in the morning, after the dew has dried. Pour the finished mixture into 4-ounce or 8-ounce bottles to share with friends.

HERBED VINEGARS

1 cup fresh herb leaves (tarragon, thyme, or a combination of basil, oregano, marjoram, and chives)

2 (6-inch-long) strips lemon rind (optional)

2 cups red or white wine vinegar (or equal parts red and white wine vinegar)

Paper coffee filter

Fresh herb sprigs (optional)

makes: 2 cups
for the fridge

hands-on time: 20 min.

total time: 2 hours, 30 min., plus 1 week chilling time

1. Wash herbs thoroughly under cold running water. Spin in a salad spinner to remove excess moisture. Pat dry with a clean towel, and gently bruise with the back of a knife. Place herbs and lemon rind, if using, in a clean 1-qt. jar or glass container.

2. Heat vinegar in a small stainless steel saucepan over medium heat 10 minutes or until bubbles appear. Pour into prepared jar, making sure herbs are completely submerged. Cool completely (about 2 hours). Cover with plastic wrap, and chill 1 week.

3. Strain vinegar mixture through a fine wire-mesh strainer lined with a paper coffee filter, and set over a large glass measuring cup. Discard solids.

4. Wash, spin, and pat dry fresh herb sprigs, if using; place in clean, dry bottles with corks or nonmetallic lids. Add strained vinegar to cover. Seal, label, and store in refrigerator up to 1 month.

Patience and white wine vinegar turn raspberries into this brilliant red elixir. The name "shrub" can refer to the mouth-pleasing drinking vinegar itself or to libations Southerners have been making with it since colonial times. Drink it straight up as a digestif. Stir a few spoonfuls into a tall glass with crushed ice and club soda for a refreshing cooler. Or add it to rum-, bourbon-, or brandy-based cocktails.

RASPBERRY SHRUB

4 cups red raspberries
1¾ cups white wine vinegar, divided

Cheesecloth
2½ to 3 cups sugar

makes: 4 (½-pt.) jars
for the shelf

hands-on time: 15 min.

total time: 12 hours, 35 min.,
plus 1 week standing time

1. Wash and drain raspberries; place in a medium glass or nonmetallic bowl with 1 cup vinegar. Crush raspberries with a fork or potato masher. Stir in remaining ¾ cup vinegar. Cover with plastic wrap, and let stand in a cool, dark place 12 hours.

2. Sterilize jars, and prepare lids as described on page 22. While jars are boiling, pour raspberry mixture into a fine wire-mesh strainer lined with 3 layers of dampened cheesecloth and placed over a large glass measuring cup. Measure liquid, and add 1⅓ cups sugar for each cup of liquid. Bring to a boil in a stainless steel saucepan, stirring until sugar dissolves. Remove from heat; let foam settle (about 1 minute). Skim off and discard any foam.

3. Pour hot liquid into hot jars, leaving ¼-inch headspace. Seal and process jars as described on pages 22–25, processing 10 minutes.

4. Remove jars from water, and let stand, undisturbed, at room temperature 24 hours. To check seals, remove the bands, and press down on the center of each lid. If the lid doesn't move, the jar is sealed. If the lid depresses and pops up again, the jar is not sealed. Store properly sealed jars in a cool, dark place up to 1 year. Refrigerate after opening, and use within 6 months.

Apple Pie

INFUSED BOURBON

Mix it Up: Pour about 1 oz. infused bourbon into
a glass with ice, and top it off with sparkling
cider, ginger ale, cola, or your favorite soft drink.

Orange, Clove, & Cranberry

INFUSED BOURBON

Combine two of your favorite things for one dynamite liqueur.

APPLE PIE-INFUSED BOURBON

1   Golden Delicious apple, chopped
2   (3-inch) cinnamon sticks
¼   tsp. ground nutmeg
1   (750-milliliter) bottle bourbon
⅓   cup sugar

1. Place first 3 ingredients in a 1-qt. canning jar. Add bourbon; cover with lid. Let bourbon stand at room temperature 4 days.

2. Shake jar to distribute flavors. Pour bourbon mixture through a fine wire-mesh strainer into a pitcher, discarding solids. Combine sugar and 3½ Tbsp. water in 1-cup microwave-safe dish. Microwave at HIGH 30 seconds. Stir until sugar is dissolved. Add to pitcher, and stir until combined. Pour into a clean 1-qt. canning jar or 3 to 4 small bottles. Seal, label, and store in refrigerator up to 2 months.

ORANGE-CLOVE-CRANBERRY-INFUSED BOURBON: Omit apple, cinnamon, and nutmeg. Place 2 (2-inch) orange rind strips, 8 whole cloves, and 1 cup lightly crushed fresh or frozen cranberries in a 1-qt. canning jar. Add bourbon; cover with metal lid, and screw on band. Let bourbon stand at room temperature 4 days. Proceed with recipe as directed in Step 2.

makes: 3¼ cups
for the fridge

hands-on time: 10 min.

total time: 15 min.,
plus 4 days standing time

SPIKED SWEET TEA

¾   cup sweetened tea
3   Tbsp. Apple Pie-Infused Bourbon or Orange-Clove-Cranberry-Infused Bourbon
1   Tbsp. fresh lemon juice
Ice
Club soda

1. Combine sweetened tea, infused bourbon, and fresh lemon juice in a cocktail shaker filled with ice. Cover with lid; shake vigorously until thoroughly chilled. Strain into a 10-oz. glass filled with ice. Top with club soda.

makes: 1¼ cups
for the table

hands-on time: 5 min.

total time: 5 min.

little jars, big flavors

This lemon liqueur, popular in Italy, is best stored in the freezer and served ice cold as an after-dinner drink. It's also quite nice in cocktails and desserts. You can substitute satsumas for the lemons and the navel orange when satsumas are in season.

LIMONCELLO

5   medium-size lemons
1   medium-size navel orange
1   (750-milliliter) bottle 190-proof
    clear grain alcohol

4   cups sugar

makes: about 4 (1-pt.) jars
for the freezer

hands-on time: 15 min.

total time: 55 min.,
plus 10 days standing time

1. Scrub fruit thoroughly; rinse well, and pat dry. Carefully remove ½ cup rind from lemons and ¼ cup rind from orange using a vegetable peeler, being careful to avoid bitter white pith. Combine rind strips and clear grain alcohol in a 1-gal. glass jar with a lid. Cover and let stand at room temperature in a cool, dark place 10 days.

2. Bring sugar and 4 cups water to a boil in a large saucepan, stirring constantly until sugar dissolves. Remove from heat, and cool slightly (10 minutes). Strain alcohol-rind mixture through a fine wire-mesh strainer into sugar-water mixture in saucepan (discard rind), and stir to combine. Cool completely (30 minutes).

3. Pour mixture into clean glass jars. Seal, label, and store in freezer up to 1 year.

ROSEMARY-LIMONCELLO JULEPS: Muddle 1 Tbsp. fresh rosemary leaves with 1 Tbsp. sugar and 1 cup Limoncello in a cocktail shaker or small bowl. Let stand 5 minutes. Strain into a pitcher, discarding solids. Stir in 2 cups each ice and club soda. Divide among glasses. Garnish with fresh rosemary sprigs. Makes: 4 cups.

This peanut-washed bourbon takes the Southern tradition of putting salted peanuts in your cola one step further. It puts the peanuts in your cocktail. The freezing and second straining help remove the peanut fat from the alcohol while leaving the peanut flavor and aroma intact.

PEANUT-WASHED BOURBON

2 cups unsalted dry-roasted peanuts

3 cups bourbon
Cheesecloth

1. Combine peanuts and bourbon in a 2-qt. glass bowl. (Peanuts should be completely covered.) Cover with plastic wrap, and let stand at room temperature 24 hours.

2. Strain through a fine wire-mesh strainer lined with 3 layers of dampened cheesecloth. Discard peanuts. Transfer strained bourbon to a 1-qt. freezer container; cover, and freeze 24 hours.

3. Strain chilled bourbon through a fine wire-mesh strainer lined with 3 layers of dampened cheesecloth. Transfer to a clean 1-qt. jar. Seal, label, and store in refrigerator up to 6 months.

PEANUT-WASHED BOURBON COCKTAIL: Stir together ¼ cup Peanut-Washed Bourbon and ½ cup cola in an ice-filled glass. Top with 1 tsp. salted, roasted peanuts. Makes: 1 cup.

makes: 2½ cups
for the fridge

hands-on time: 5 min.

total time: 5 min.,
plus 2 days standing time

little jars, big flavors

This fruity infused vodka is a girls-night-in waiting to happen. Sip straight up or with equal portions of orange juice and club soda over ice.

POMEGRANATE-PINEAPPLE VODKA

2 cups (½-inch) cubed fresh pineapple	1½ cups 80-proof vodka
1½ cups fresh pomegranate seeds	Cheesecloth

makes: 2¼ cups for the fridge

hands-on time: 20 min.

total time: 2 hours, 20 min., plus 3 days standing time

1. Place 1 cup pineapple and ¾ cup pomegranate seeds in each of 2 (1-qt.) jars. Pour ¾ cup vodka over fruit in each jar. Cover jars with lids, and let stand at room temperature 3 days, swirling fruit mixture in jars occasionally.

2. Line a fine wire-mesh strainer with 3 layers of dampened cheesecloth. Place strainer over a bowl. Pour fruit mixture into strainer. (Discard fruit.) Pour strained vodka into a clean (1-qt.) jar or other glass container with a lid. Seal, label, and store in refrigerator up to 6 months.

NOTE: Be sure to wash fruit rind before cutting into fruit and to trim off and discard any blemished pieces of fruit. To remove seeds from pomegranate, score skin and break fruit into quarters. Working over a bowl, tap skin side of quarters with a wooden spoon, knocking seeds loose and into bowl.

Take a note from Southern bartenders, and raid the pantry to mix up some of your own special bitters. Used in cocktails and to add a little somethin'-somethin' to baked goods, stews, and coffee drinks, these fragrant bitters also make fabulous gifts.

SPICED PECAN-COFFEE BITTERS

¾ cup chopped pecans
¾ cup medium-roast coffee beans
3 cups bourbon or whiskey
2 tsp. cassia chips

1 tsp. organic wild cherry bark
½ tsp. dried grated lemon peel
Cheesecloth
3 Tbsp. sorghum syrup

makes: 5 (½-cup) jars
for the shelf

hands-on time: 35 min.

total time: 35 min.,
plus 13 days standing time

NOTE: Look for wild cherry bark at natural foods stores or online.

1. Preheat oven to 350°. Bake pecans in a single layer in a shallow pan 5 to 8 minutes or until toasted and fragrant, stirring halfway through.

2. Place coffee beans in a zip-top plastic freezer bag; seal. Lightly crush or crack beans using a rolling pin or a heavy skillet. Combine coffee beans, toasted pecans, bourbon, and next 3 ingredients in a clean 1-qt. canning jar or other nonreactive container with lid. Cover and let steep out of direct sunlight at room temperature 10 days, shaking the jar once a day.

3. Pour mixture through a wire-mesh strainer lined with 6 layers of cheesecloth into a large bowl. Wash jar; return mixture to clean, dry jar. Add sorghum syrup; cover with lid, and shake well. Let stand out of direct sunlight at room temperature 3 days.

4. Pour into ½-cup jars or bottles, if desired. Seal, label, and store at room temperature up to 1 year.

Can't locate a cocktail shaker? Use a canning jar to shake up this tasty cocktail.

SOUTHERN TIRAMISÙ MARTINI

2	tsp. sugar
½	tsp. Spiced Pecan-Coffee Bitters (previous page)
¼	cup dark rum, divided
2	Tbsp. heavy cream
1½	cups cracked ice

Sweetened cocoa powder

1. Muddle sugar, bitters, and a splash of rum in a cocktail shaker or canning jar. Add remaining rum, heavy cream, and cracked ice. Cover and shake vigorously. Strain into chilled martini glass. Let cream rise. Dust lightly with cocoa.

NOTE: We tested with Ghirardelli Sweet Ground Chocolate and Cocoa for the sweetened cocoa powder.

makes: 1 serving for the table

hands-on time: 5 min.

total time: 5 min.

Southern boiled peanuts typically take all day on the stove-top, but this slow-cooker recipe makes them easy. Start them before bedtime, and they'll be ready for the freezer or for tailgating the next afternoon. Though you eat only the nuts inside, it's traditional to serve boiled peanuts in their shells.

GEORGIA-STYLE BOILED PEANUTS

2   lb. raw peanuts, in shell   1   cup salt

1. Combine peanuts, salt, and 12 cups water in a 5- or 6-qt. slow cooker. Cover and cook on HIGH 18 hours or until peanuts are soft. Drain peanuts before serving or storing. Store in zip-top plastic freezer bags in the refrigerator up to 2 weeks or in the freezer up to 2 months. Reheat in the microwave before serving.

CAJUN BOILED PEANUTS: Reduce salt to ¾ cup, and add 1 (3-oz.) package boil-in-bag shrimp and crab boil and ⅓ to ½ cup hot sauce to slow cooker before cooking.

makes: 18 cups for
the fridge or the freezer

hands-on time: 5 min.

total time: 18 hours, 5 min.

Boiled peanuts stand in for chickpeas in this flavorful Southern take on the Mediterranean dip.

BOILED PEANUT HUMMUS

1   cup thawed shelled Georgia-Style or Cajun Boiled Peanuts (previous page)
2   Tbsp. tahini
2   Tbsp. fresh lemon juice
1   Tbsp. chopped fresh parsley
1   tsp. minced fresh garlic
¼   tsp. ground cumin
Pinch of ground red pepper
2   Tbsp. olive oil
Garnishes: olive oil, roasted peanuts
Carrot and celery sticks, halved radishes, and pita chips

1. Process first 7 ingredients in a food processor until coarsely chopped, stopping to scrape down sides. With processor running, pour olive oil through food chute in a slow, steady stream, processing until mixture is smooth. Stir in up to 5 Tbsp. water, 1 Tbsp. at a time, for desired spreading consistency. Serve with vegetables and pita chips. Garnish, if desired.

makes: 1 cup for the table

hands-on time: 15 min.

total time: 15 min.

little jars, big flavors

This mustard is tangy and spicy. It'll blow your hair back but won't blow your head off. Fear not: The food processor does not completely puree the mustard. It helps produce a creamy mustard with lots of whole seeds.

WHOLE-GRAIN MUSTARD

1¼ cups white wine vinegar (5% acidity), divided

1¼ cups red wine vinegar (5% acidity), divided

¾ cup brown mustard seeds

¾ cup yellow mustard seeds

¼ cup dry white wine

2 Tbsp. honey

2½ Tbsp. dry mustard

4 tsp. salt

2 tsp. freshly ground pepper

makes: 4 (½-pt.) jars for the shelf

hands-on time: 20 min.

total time: 45 min., plus 10 days standing time

1. Stir together 1 cup white wine vinegar, 1 cup red wine vinegar, and brown and yellow mustard seeds in a clean 1-qt. jar. Cover with lid, and let stand at room temperature 5 days, adding more red or white vinegar if seeds look dry.

2. Stir in remaining ¼ cup white wine vinegar and ¼ cup red wine vinegar, white wine, and honey. Stir in dry mustard. Cover with lid, and let stand at room temperature 5 more days. (Mixture will be bubbly.)

3. Process mustard mixture, salt, and pepper in a food processor 1½ minutes or until slightly creamy, stopping to scrape down sides.

4. Sterilize jars, and prepare lids as described on page 22.

5. Fill, seal, and process jars as described on pages 22–25, leaving ¼-inch headspace and processing 15 minutes.

6. Remove jars from water, and let stand, undisturbed, at room temperature 24 hours. To check seals, remove the bands, and press down on the center of each lid. If the lid doesn't move, the jar is sealed. If the lid depresses and pops up again, the jar is not sealed. Store properly sealed jars in a cool, dark place up to 1 year. Refrigerate after opening.

METRIC EQUIVALENTS

The recipes that appear in this cookbook use the standard U.S. method for measuring liquid and dry or solid ingredients (teaspoons, tablespoons, and cups). The information on this chart is provided to help cooks outside the United States successfully use these recipes. All equivalents are approximate.

Metric Equivalents for Different Types of Ingredients

A standard cup measure of a dry or solid ingredient will vary in weight depending on the type of ingredient. A standard cup of liquid is the same volume for any type of liquid. Use the following chart when converting standard cup measures to grams (weight) or milliliters (volume).

Standard Cup	Fine Powder (ex. flour)	Grain (ex. rice)	Granular (ex. sugar)	Liquid Solids (ex. butter)	Liquid (ex. milk)
1	140 g	150 g	190 g	200 g	240 ml
¾	105 g	113 g	143 g	150 g	180 ml
⅔	93 g	100 g	125 g	133 g	160 ml
½	70 g	75 g	95 g	100 g	120 ml
⅓	47 g	50 g	63 g	67 g	80 ml
¼	35 g	38 g	48 g	50 g	60 ml
⅛	18 g	19 g	24 g	25 g	30 ml

Useful Equivalents for Liquid Ingredients by Volume

¼ tsp					=		1 ml
½ tsp					=		2 ml
1 tsp					=		5 ml
3 tsp	=	1 Tbsp		=	½ fl oz	=	15 ml
		2 Tbsp	= ⅛ cup	=	1 fl oz	=	30 ml
		4 Tbsp	= ¼ cup	=	2 fl oz	=	60 ml
		5⅓ Tbsp	= ⅓ cup	=	3 fl oz	=	80 ml
		8 Tbsp	= ½ cup	=	4 fl oz	=	120 ml
		10⅔ Tbsp	= ⅔ cup	=	5 fl oz	=	160 ml
		12 Tbsp	= ¾ cup	=	6 fl oz	=	180 ml
		16 Tbsp	= 1 cup	=	8 fl oz	=	240 ml
		1 pt	= 2 cups	=	16 fl oz	=	480 ml
		1 qt	= 4 cups	=	32 fl oz	=	960 ml
					33 fl oz	=	1000 ml = 1 l

Useful Equivalents for Dry Ingredients by Weight

(To convert ounces to grams, multiply the number of ounces by 30.)

1 oz	=	1/16 lb	=	30 g
4 oz	=	¼ lb	=	120 g
8 oz	=	½ lb	=	240 g
12 oz	=	¾ lb	=	360 g
16 oz	=	1 lb	=	480 g

Useful Equivalents for Length

(To convert inches to centimeters, multiply the number of inches by 2.5.)

1 in				=	2.5 cm	
6 in	= ½ ft			=	15 cm	
12 in	= 1 ft			=	30 cm	
36 in	= 3 ft	= 1 yd		=	90 cm	
40 in				=	100 cm	= 1 m

Useful Equivalents for Cooking/Oven Temperatures

	Fahrenheit	Celsius	Gas Mark
Freeze water	32° F	0° C	
Room temperature	68° F	20° C	
Boil water	212° F	100° C	
Bake	325° F	160° C	3
	350° F	180° C	4
	375° F	190° C	5
	400° F	200° C	6
	425° F	220° C	7
	450° F	230° C	8
Broil			Grill

INDEX

CANNING RESOURCES & REFERENCES

While making this book, we learned a lot from the following sources. You might, too.

• The U.S. Department of Agriculture's *Complete Guide to Home Canning* covers everything from basic canning procedures and ingredient selection to tested recipes for boiling-water and pressure canning. It's available in several free downloadable sections at nchfp.uga.edu/publications/publications_usda.html.

• The National Center for Home Food Preservation at The University of Georgia in Athens, and its website (nchfp.uga.edu) offer a wealth of information for the home canner, including fact sheets, frequently asked questions, tested recipes for boiling-water canning, pressure canning, and other forms of food preservation.

• Freshpreserving.com, the website of canning product maker Ball, offers oodles of information on jars, lids, and pectin, as well as troubleshooting advice in the event things just don't work out.

• If you're interested in developing your own canned recipes within acceptable pH guidelines, the Oklahoma State University Food and Agricultural Products Center has an excellent factsheet on choosing and using a pH meter. The curious can find it here: fapc.okstate.edu/files/factsheets/fapc117.pdf.

◆

about the photos

Technique shot (page 28), and Bread-and-Butter Pickles (page 143) by **Cedric Angeles** for *Southern Living;* Apple Pie-Infused Bourbon (pages 234–235) by **Jennifer Davick** for *Southern Living;* Herbed Vinegars (page 230) by **Beth Dreiling-Hontzas** for *Southern Living;* Strawberry-Basil Jam (page 40) by **Hélène Dujardin** for Oxmoor House; technique shots and stills (pages 13–26) by **Becky Luigart-Stayner** for Oxmoor House; Vanilla Bean-Pineapple-Sage Layer Cake (page 87 and back cover), Blueberry-Raspberry Freezer Jam and Blueberry-Raspberry Steel-Cut Oats (pages 200–201), Strawberry-Rhubarb Banana Smoothies (pages 206–207), Peppery Texas Freezer Pickles (pages 212), Chicken Pasta with Pesto Cream Sauce (pages 216–217), Blueberry Syrup (page 222), Peach-Vanilla Syrup (page 225), and Rhubarb and Rose Water Syrup (page 226) by **Daniel Taylor** for Oxmoor House; all others by **Ellen Silverman** for Oxmoor House.

about the recipes

Strawberry-Basil Jam (page 41), Scuppernong Jelly (page 54), and Chunky Lemon-Fig Preserves (page 82) by **Rebecca Lang**. All others by *Southern Living* and Oxmoor House staff and contributors.

special thanks

To **Kathleen Royal Phillips**, canner extraordinaire, for styling the majority of the food pictured in this book, and to **Claire Cormany, Sarah Doss, Sara Lyon, Leah McLaughlin, Emily Robinson,** and **Leah Van Deren** for lending their time and their beautiful hands to the putting-up party and technique photo shoots.